STONEWALL INN EDITIONS
Keith Kahla, General Editor

WEST OF YESTERDAY,
EAST OF SUMMER

WEST OF YESTERDAY, EAST OF SUMMER

NEW AND SELECTED POEMS
(1973–1993)

Paul Monette

x

x

x

x

x

x

ST. MARTIN'S PRESS
NEW YORK

Library of Congress Cataloging-in-Publication Data

Monette, Paul.
    West of yesterday, east of summer : new and selected
poems / Paul Monette.
        p.   cm.
    ISBN 0-312-13616-1
    1. Gay men—United States—Poetry.   I. Title.
[PS3563.0523W47   1995]
811'.54—dc20   95-30300
                                                  CIP

First Stonewall Inn Edition: October 1995
        10 9 8 7 6 5 4 3 2

ACKNOWLEDGMENTS

The Carpenter at the Asylum was originally published by Little, Brown and Company (1975).

"Contexts" first appeared in *The Yale Literary Magazine*.

No Witnesses was originally published by Avon Books (1981).

"My Shirts" first appeared in *Christopher Street*.

"Bones and Jewels" first appeared in *Shenandoah*. It received the Coordinating Council of Literary Magazines Award for Best Poem in 1977.

"The Wedding Letter" first appeared in *Poetry*.

"Musical Comedy" first appeared in *Orpheus*.

Love Alone: 18 Elegies for Rog was originally published by St. Martin's Press (1988), thanks to the good graces and great enthusiasm of Norman Laurila.

"The Worrying" first appeared in *American Poetry Review*.

Love Alone received the first Words Project for AIDS Award in 1989.

Several of the *New Poems* first appeared in *Poets for Life: Seventy-six Poets Respond to AIDS*, published by Crown Publishers, Inc. (1990). They included "Buckley," "Waiting to Die," "40," "To GB from Tuscany" and "Ed Dying."

"Committing to Memory" and "Stephen at the FDA" first appeared in *Frontiers*.

"The Bee-Eater" first appeared in *The Threepenny Review*, thanks to Wendy Lesser.

No Witnesses and *Love Alone* could not have been completed without the support and encouragement of a pair of Ingram-Merrill Foundation grants, which the author gratefully acknowledges.

The enthusiasm and dedication of Michael Denneny at St. Martin's Press was crucial to the shaping of *Love Alone*, as well as that of the text in hand. Michael has my undying thanks and brotherly love for his acuity in understanding what I was trying to do before I understood it myself.

And finally, an affectionate thank-you to Barbara Horwitz for her constant support throughout the compiling of this volume. But then she has already secured her place in the heart's circle of this queer's chosen family.

CONTENTS

No Witnesses (1981)

The Carpenter at the Asylum (1975)

INTRODUCTION

A BACKWARD LOOK

It is surely beyond a truism that all young men are convinced they're immortal. Never a more ambiguous gift than it is today in the United States of Guns, as kids dodge drive-by shootings and gang justice, buffeted by the hormonal tornado of midadolescence, too cocky to wear their rubbers in the rain. Not so in the sluggish daze of *my* youth—those stillborn fifties—when I was too timid to cast a shadow and lived in the airless vault of the closet.

But full of my own immortal longings, even then. For you see, I was going to be a Poet, so that before I was twenty my progress into the ranks of the timeless was set in stone. I could practically smell the ink of my own canonization: *Selected Poems, Collected Poems, The Complete Poems,* and then of course the bio and the *Letters.* I never wavered in that certainty of the march to greatness, though I daresay wavering was all I ever did otherwise in life.

Blissfully uncritical. Of course I never wrote anything except about myself, but then it was all so *serious* and dark that it fairly stank with merit. What Anne Sexton used to call "a fever chart for a bad case of melancholy"—and she was genuinely brilliant at it, so naked and so self-lacerating she could make you flinch from the page. Whereas my own histrionic locutions were all in the service of constructing the Big Lie: that this paragon of eloquent despair was as hetero as the next guy, but terminally wounded, however obscurely. Which is not to say I wasn't in real pain, and yet without a clue that its *expression* was a numbing round of obfuscation and cliché.

And still the shelf of immortality beckoned: *Selected, Collected, Complete.* Rather like Auntie Mame in the throes of the autobiography she hasn't written a word of yet: "I see it in two volumes—boxed, like Proust." When what I ought to have paid attention to instead was Wordsworth's bone-chilling assessment of his fatal vocation:

> *We Poets in our youth begin in gladness;*
> *But thereof comes in the end despondency*
> *and madness.*

And the key word is *thereof*, of course. As if the gladder you are at the start—coltish and irrepressible, brimming with the *mot juste*—to that very degree the Muse will turn and fuck you in the end.

All of which is rather more prelude than my slim little first book warrants. But remember, nobody's read *The Carpenter at the Asylum* for going on twenty years now, not unless they've managed to pick one up in an Olde Curiosity bookshop. Reading the poems through again has left my face in a semipermanent wince, for I can see all the seams and the dropped stitches. The curious mix of vast pretension—*I've read everything, so there*—and the cultivation of obscurity to a level approaching the pathological.

Still, I've managed to salvage four that don't embarrass me—poems that have a certain dogged merit for aspiring with such passion toward the Beautiful. Beauty as a goal for its own sake, the more removed from earthly dross the better. It's true that *Contexts*—being a primer on how to become a poet—hides its real agenda, hid it even from me at the time. In fact it's a crush poem, for a student I determined not to fall in love with, a resounding failure in that regard. Dedicated now to David Schorr, my oldest friend and fellow artist, who knows the stakes and the score of the heart's journey as well as I.

By the time I started to work on the set of dramatic monologues that would come together in *No Witnesses*, I had suffered a sea change. Most evident in the poem that begins the present selection. *My Shirts* was written in the flush of the first month after I met Roger—September 1974—the touchstone moment after which nothing would ever be the same again. At last, a chance to write a love poem for real, no gender blur required.

The Wedding Letter was composed the following summer, as a most ambiguous epithalamion for my brother and sister-in-law, two people I love to the depths of my being, though you wouldn't know it from the savage dementia of Hansel's epistle. I was under the influence of Bettelheim's *The Uses of Enchantment*, and sought to identify myself with Hansel's darkest secret. Gretel, he says, who actually dispatched the witch, has managed to grow up without any lingering guilt or nightmares. While Hansel has clung to the psychic damage as to a raft in a whirlwind, finding his way back to the burnedout candyhouse in the woods. I meant his journey to stand, I think, for the derangement of the closet, the curse of being different.

The two monologues included here—*Bones and Jewels* and *Musical Comedy*—represented a kind of breaking of the bonds of the lyric poem. Much affected by the exquisite *Two-Part Inventions* of Richard Howard, I wanted to bring to bear all the elements of narrative and drama. The encounter between Edna St. Vincent Millay and Edmund Wilson is based on an actual incident from the twenties, when Millay had achieved a fame of near-Madonna proportions. Wilson asked her to marry him, and instead of answering she fled to her mother and sister in Truro on the dunes of Cape Cod. There I imagined the courting dance of the two literary giants.

I read in a Coward biography that at the height of his own Broadway triumph, he headed by train overland to California—a three-day journey that afforded the bi-coastal a nice break from the general frenzy of showbiz. Famously, Coward had written the whole of *Hay Fever* on such a cross-country passage, so glib and elegant and facile was his style that he could pick it up like knitting. At the time I had as serious an aspiration to cultivate a voice like his as I'd ever had for Wallace Stevens or Frost.

I conceived it as an epistolary drama. Five letters mailed from various depots along the way, all addressed to Coward's glamorous buddy Marlene Dietrich. He's promised to write a song for her while in transit, something on the order of *Falling in Love Again*, about which she'd written the book.

Then the deus ex machina arrives, in the person of a veiled mysterious stranger who boards the train in the middle of nowhere. Who turns out to be Garbo. I must have spent four or five months in the composition, flat-out loving the chance to write dialogue for such a contrary pair. I remember finishing the piece on a Trailways bus between Hyannis Port and Boston, where I'd gone to spend the night with Roger, who was attending an annual meeting of a corporate client. At that point we only had one car between us.

What I wrote on the bus was the final song, *Home on the Southport Car*. At the time I didn't realize it represented my valedictory to poetry. For months I read it to anyone who'd listen—a small group at best, patient enough to sit through five hundred lines of glib. I tinkered with other poems for a while, especially something about Aladdin, but my heart wasn't in it. By midsummer my friend Gert Macy—seventy then, and bearing the glorious lineage of her work with Katharine Cornell and Martha Graham—was assuring me *Musical Comedy* was brilliant. "But really, who's going to read it? Who's the audience?" To her I think it seemed like a waste of breath, if not talent, to be writing for the minuscule band of the faithful who read poetry for pleasure—and not just fellow poets poring over each other to check out the competition.

That innocent question of Gert's—innocent, ha!—happened to dovetail with my receiving a grant from the Ingram-Merrill Foundation, ostensibly to pull *Musical Comedy* into a book. But I started a novel instead, and frankly never looked back at the castle-in-the-sky where poetry held court.

There were hard times in the next several years, especially when I was trying to pacify some felt need in the publishing world to "lean a little more mainstream." And during those awful troughs between screenplays as I waited for the studio execs to debase and expunge all original ideas before I'd written so much as a comma. Why waste a draft that didn't respect the paint-by-numbers ethos? Those were the times when Roger would venture, ever so gently: "Why don't you write some poems? You know, you're very good at it."

A big step forward for him, by the way, who hadn't really responded to the baroque effulgence of my early work, all that buried feeling. He preferred the plain-spoken eloquence of his friend Jean Follain, the epigrammatic pith of J. V. Cunningham, and, for exaltedness, the heightened passion of Rilke. I was too chatty and all-over-the-board for his taste. But he meant it when he would ask me to take a turn at verse again—nonjudgmental as ever, but fearing, I think, that I was squandering the difficult gift of going straight for the heart.

Usually I just pooh-poohed it, saying that there was more than enough poetry written and lying unread for me to need to add to the pile. And then one night in a bad time—when I felt I was writing high-priced memos for the sort of cruel vulgarian who was in it for the Peruvian flake and the bimbos—Roger made his mild suggestion yet again. We were walking the dog in the canyon, the end of all our days. And I surprised even myself by the gravity and fervor of my reaction.

"Don't wish for it, Rog. If I really went back to poetry, it would be because of some terrible tragedy, so awful I couldn't do anything else."

When was that exactly—'80, '81? By which time the incomprehensible nightmare had already seeded and taken root in a million of our brothers, invisible still.

I don't really believe I was being psychic there so much as I had a superstitious feel for what they could do to a writer. Osip Mandelstam dead in his prime in a Stalinist labor camp. Ezra Pound in the wire cage in the prison yard, writing the *Pisan Cantos*. Poets in war and poets in pain, the inconsolable grief and the slow disintegration of terminal illness. Don't wish that on me, please.

And when it came to pass, it turned out to be all the calamities rolled into one. Within days of Roger's diagnosis I was paralyzed—as if I could no longer hold a pen, let alone write with it. Six or eight months later, in the second year of Roger's dying, I began to make furious drafts composed of pain and rage, trying to think nothing at all. Eventually two or three of them wouldn't leave me alone, demanding obsessive revision, taking their place among the *New Poems*—*Buckley* for one, and the Nureyev poem. But then I never really thought of them as poetry either, which probably kept them clean.

No day went by when I didn't recite to myself as a kind of mantra Randall Jarrell's *reductio* on the horror of being human:

> . . . *nothing comes from nothing,*
> *The darkness from the darkness. Pain comes from*
> *the darkness*
> *And we call it wisdom. It is pain.** *

The only one that was more or less finished by the final weeks of Roger's life was *The Supreme Pork*, in part

*Randall Jarrell, *The Complete Poems* (Farrar, Straus; 1969), from *90 North*, page 114.

because he'd been so appalled by the Court's 8–1 majority in *Bowers* v. *Hardwick*. Blind by then, he had me read to him from the *Times* the whole of Justice Blackmun's dissent. He talked about it for days whenever one of his lawyer friends would call. Roger was the one who made me understand that a great dissent could over the course of time acquire the moral force to alter bigoted laws that seemed impregnable.

So the poem was rather a gift of outrage to try to assuage the aggrieved honor of my beloved, who could not believe the Court had sunk so far. I read it to him one afternoon in bed, as he lay curled against the fever, facing the garden he could no longer see. (In the same position I've lain curled myself these last seven weeks, laid low by a laundry list of symptoms and indignities, and thirteen hours of I.V. treatment every day.) I ripped through my recitation with unpunctuated force and when I got to the end there was silence. I thought maybe he'd fallen asleep.

Then he spoke with a soft astonishment. "Sweetheart, that's terrific. How can you say you'll never write again?"

For that's *exactly* what I'd say, lying in his arms late at night, sobbing as if my heart would break. "I can't do it without you," I'd say. "Yes, you can," came the soothing reply. "And besides, I'm still here."

But then five weeks later he wasn't anymore, and I figured I'd died too. His doctor's admonition the night he died—"You have to write about him, Paul"—was just so much empty advice. Then, it must have been two weeks later, I was standing watch at the grave in Forest Lawn, as I did every day while dusk fell. Next morning I had to leave for Boston to visit my parents, who hadn't seen me in a year and a half, dreading every minute of the further separation from Roger.

And I suddenly realized that if the plane went down tomorrow, there would be no record anywhere of what we'd suffered and how love got us through. So I sat in the grass in the failing light and opened my journal and scribbled about twenty-five lines—the poem called

Here—and that night I propped it on my desk, labeled *To Whom It May Concern.*

The next day on the plane to Boston I pulled out the journal again, and wrote the whole of *No Goodbyes*, in a torrent of unfiltered feeling. And that is how they were all written from then on, at least the first ten, entirely *without thinking.* An endless catalogue of the lost, nothing too minor to heave onto the pyre of my dead days. I don't doubt that some shaping imagination was at work, even so, but it stayed resolutely unconscious, completely on its own. I had no sense that anyone *else* would want them, but I hadn't counted on the luck of its crossing the desk of Michael Denneny, who was ready to go to contract with only half the poems in place.

The volume appeared in March of 1988, and when the first copy appeared by overnight express, I sat at my desk sobbing and saying over and over, "Rog, we did it." Whatever intrinsic merit the elegies had, I'd accomplished what I set out to do, leaving a record of our love and times. It was in the nature of an unexpected bonus that so many people responded enthusiastically to the work—not put off or bewildered as we feared by the run-on frenzy of the style, the banishing of punctuation. Moreover, I even got my wish as I had stated it in the Preface. That the readership proved to be drawn from the ranks of the AIDS-afflicted and the grief-haunted, and not from that plucky little band of the general poetry reader.

But that wasn't nearly as odd as the reaction of the general poetry *writer.* For old times' sake, I sent out eight or ten copies to my colleagues from a decade ago, most of whose work I'd loyally kept up with—despite its being the opposite of mine. So perhaps I shouldn't have been so surprised by the responses. Two poets wrote back nearly identical letters, in which they dismissed *Love Alone* as "not being poetry at all, really. Too raw and too unfiltered, and of course riddled with clichés." But clearly an important "document," all the same.

"It's clearly more like performance art, isn't it? Have you thought of showing it to Eric Bogosian?"

And my favorite. "Thank you for the book, with that wonderful picture of you and Roger on the cover. I'll cherish it. The text, I'm afraid, is not my thing."

I can only imagine what the silver-tongued response will be to the body of *New Poems*. Too political by a mile, unbearably strident, nothing reflected on, no *form*. Well, at least they've got all that right. Raw being just how AIDS has left me, flayed of layers of skin I didn't know I had—flayed to the bone—I was screaming as much as composing when I sat to write. Pain was pain, not wisdom, and the idea of waxing metaphorical and philosophical about such horrors seemed at best presumptuous, at worst insulting. So if I have succeeded in convincing the mainstream run of poets—with their Guggenheims and their tenure tracks, with their sure-footed march to *Selected, Collected, Complete*—that I mean to stay an outsider, lobbing my poems like pipe bombs, so be it.

One thing is abundantly clear. The difference between the first half of my career (the nice part) and the war work of AIDS is like two sides of a chasm, with no rope bridge connecting. AIDS is the great cleave in the world, and nothing will ever be the same again. I'm glad I was able to take my stand with the suffering and the banished. I owe no less to the myriad comrades I have lost, and I don't have to be "nice" to anyone. Let's make some noise, as I tell Stephen in the foxhole love poem that finishes off these *New Poems*. Noise and bad manners and satire blunt as the *Dunciad*. Definitely not for sissies.

NEW POEMS

(1987–1993)

To Victor Brown
unshakable witness

COMMITTING TO MEMORY

FOR WINSTON

I

Have you thought of this: that we already
live in Durango just below Wolf Pass
because it was our idea. Snowmelt
roars in the meadow, and the mudroom
off the kitchen is thick as potter's clay.
Dreaming eagles crisscross the Divide,
going east or west by the merest flick
of air, all the same to them or us.
In the stable an Appaloosa and a paint
still wait to be ridden and named,
and the tack room—through the low door there—
stocked like a rusty toybox. No point
in having so much rope unless you can
tie a knot. It has to hold. Like the poppies
rioting yellow on every cliff edge
memorizing fast their one day open wide
west of yesterday, east of summer,
holding on for life to such high places
as we live, the difficult house of joy.

II

If it was swimming it would be swimming
so far down the coral spiral where ink
and lava merge that the dome in the reef
would be the tip of Atlantis, first room
of the lost kingdom, dolphins cavorting.
Except it isn't swimming either, not really,
despite the ocean it rivers us into.
This much for the vessel though: till now
always needing a ship to be a sailor,
I find I cross more water these days
in our room, beached on a sand bar, wrecked
in time. Between Crete and Ithaca,
sirens wailing *go ahead do it*, I'm lashed
to the mast like Ulysses, I forget why,

but the punishment nicely fits the crime—
twenty lashes, twenty of the best.
When I first saw you I thought you must be
looking at someone else, somebody you
were meeting at a station. You looked so glad
to have the man behind me home again,
as if you would carry all his baggage
till he was weightless. The way you carry
mine now, for I was the one getting off.
How did you know I'd been traveling
in circles, gone so long there was no one
left to fetch me? Gone so long avoiding
the water you seemed a sort of mirage
until I drank you. Let alone this ocean
wild with sirens, a raft in a whirlpool
for our bed, spinning at anchor, drownproof.
As to rank, if it's okay I'll be a pirate.
You be captain—so long as you show me how
to navigate a dream that goes this deep.

III

Sometimes like Vincent and his burning sky
I'm so far out of myself I'm
a cypress, clanging a thousand green
bells. Especially now with the solstice
coming on, druidical and perm-frosted,
we crave a chill in the air who have been
sunstruck too long. What you must remember
is the reason we are on fire like this
is to light our way to New Year's. Nobody
knows how many are lost, how many more
will follow. There is the narrowest zone
between the ices of winter and the deep
freeze of the black chamber. Nevertheless,
here is where we have to skate, waltzing
on a sheet of ice membrane-thin. Enough
of summer. Give me the smoke of your breath,
this longest night with the stars erupting,
kin to those priests of the waning sun

dancing in their stone circles. Didn't we
meet on the brink of winter? So, give us
bare branches and birds thronging south,
a great horned owl on our telephone pole.
We'll fuck in the snow and come in for tea,
safe in the winter harbor of the heart.
Druid brother, pagan mate, ours be the hard
flame, ours the silver fields of frost
and a pair of cypresses crowning the hill,
reaching to graze the sky. Men can love like that.

THE SUPREME PORK

is not ready for dick which is bad news
for cowboys shroud the bunkhouse mirrors guys
shower room's off limits so is sweat
i.e. you can't eat it you can still sweat
but nicely and by yourself don't eat bupkes
is the general rule ride alone Injustice
Rehnquist speaking for the Pork neglects to
mention the seethe of maggots riced like a
wedding in his puffed Orwellian gown
he proposes the Rule of Thumb where dick is
contraindicated Cuban jails so deep
they debouch in China and no men kiss in
the bottommost cells their lips are shriven
away how else will they ever get straight
exactly where the thing does not belong
not to mention their butts nonfunctional
in highchurch whites where's the fag JDL
when you need it the exfundamentalists
ripple through the land like an underground
railway hiding up trees and gazing in
at the j.v. wrestlers pacing their bedrooms
can't talk to the coach can't leave it alone
how in hell does one man ever tag up
with his dream numero if it sucks and
bungs the wrong hole love is an outlaw thang
what did they do for fun you wonder in
Gomorrah sell Amway meanwhile why has
Georgia not passed a law against me I
freely admit I'd fuck the tanktop of
a dirt-blond over-the-hill Melrose waiter
my fly is an open book what's legal
in Georgia anyway high colonics Sherle
Wagner bidets with swan faucets baptist
Jockeys never show a proper shitline
oh even as I write let there be this
one poem banned in Georgia and bring all
the five injustices down for a burning books
and videorapes and the too long single

for piggily wiggily hogfat overflows
the inkwells of the Pork and Jesus is hetero
and not a hunk tiny figged-over peeny
and the fair state peaked on the brow of a hill
high on the ultramarine Aegean is still
and only a broken pediment ashed in the rain
being gotten wrong by shyster lawyers
scales all tipped and rusty it seems the Pork
will see us cowpokes hang by our balls to
keep the civilians in rubber shorts and bibs
justitia huic huac semper fi non homo
homo scored in Latin above the door
which no one now may open the only way to fuck
is straight up straight in eyes shut tight

Written in protest of the Pork's decision in *Bowers* v. *Hard-wick*, upholding the sodomy laws in Georgia; by way of spray-painting the lie that's etched in the pediment, *Equal Justice Under The Law*; and in honor of the dissenting opinion of Justice Blackmun, the last of the just.

oh boy oh boy four years to go before
Robert Louis Stevenson dies in Samoa
gimme four more and I'll get a degree
in Greek statues I'll learn Chinese be kind
to my dearest enemies lady lady
save us a dance it's coming down in sheets
out there rivers of frangipani white
clouded peaks the cold volcanoes oh please
be kind to us who are not kidnapped save
by demons we father forth 40's half
a death these days World War I all over
the flower of a generation gone
to bits in Flanders like a rugby match
gone haywire all the poets gunned and buttered
till only Shaw was left to grow up and
Rebecca West grew barren as the wives
of ancient Thebes and life sucked no more tea
look the UN is 40 and solves nothing
and I saw day ten weeks after the light
show at Hiroshima and also solved
nothing ask any phobic it's not the heights
it's the edges that get you that weird thing
of being drawn to the precipice do it
the time has come to take the plunge and none
of your youthly coy and basket shots will
save you time doesn't give a fuck oh but
we planned such plans if the war hadn't come
and the weather had held and life had cleared
like a late Manet the Scot died half a world
from the cinder choke of his native damp
and so will I bone-thin and sunburned blown
like a sailor take my slot in the coral
chambers still if I must be me not him
no buccaneer silver Jekyll and Hyde
to make me fit for a boy to read if I
must go early give me please one friend one

year but nothing's enough and the cliffs at Thera
where the old world ended tomorrow my love
is a stolen kiss but we sail together
if we sail at all hey 40's kid stuff

NUREYEV DOESN'T HAVE AIDS

or so they say but the season's still off
at least in Paris and all her colonies
as to what to do after dance the gun-
runner Rimbaud is the paradigm post-
art position a little border war
khaki and goat kebabs no mail till the *fin*
de siècle is safely passed if the feet die
first you must sit out the millennium
not please God with those Gorey vampire queens
trading tights on the lilac market skip
Zaire ten million and counting skip the drought
ditto Pretoria Regency flats and Liszt
not the E ride among the starved these days
no condo Rudy no IRA no golf
you retire from godhead by getting lost
trade your 80 curtain calls for the zebra
savannahs the moss headwaters where Leakey's
5-toes first walked upright and remember
even Rimbaud reached for his Mont Blanc sometimes
body count penny cards guerrilla demands
you catch the drift the season in hell starts
after say one day you're cutting a deal
with mudcake warriors trading bullets for
amber beads it's all very Jean Gabin
till some kid slips a red ant up your shorts
and you quick feint to a Chaplin two-step
then skitter off on a tango Valentino
dancing with your M-16 they hold their swollen
bellies and shriek you're a god again Fred
and Ginger all in one and the pocks on your
buttermilk skin are only the kiss of death
cause everyone's already got it the whole
world's sinking like a hippo in ooze it takes
a dancing man to cure the boondocks deep in
the penicillin jungle one good Paris leap
and you're Apollo aloft in his dazzling cars

DR. BURNOUT

is not in he's taking the afternoon off
to trade his black Ferrari for a red
he will not entertain another bruise
a cough is non-specific we no longer
diagnose we prefer to refer Dr.
dreamed last night of a gold-green apple just
the sort that conked Newton nature is not
to blame for ripeness falls or the ice cracks
of a zero year but here is the thing about
dreams the gold became a dollar in Dr.'s
pocket the green green apple sat on the head
of Dr.'s beloved daffy as a Magritte
nurse will show you where to leave your wallet
strip to the bone surely you see a cure
is not productive what we do best is test
leech here pentagram there the old magic
makes the rain think how the medicine men
of the Maya tore out the hearts of warrior
virgins and cured the national headache
no wonder Dr.'s always had the prettiest
hut with the pearly view of the humid gulf
in the Lascaux caves he had the corner by
the fire ate veal chops and tiny carrots
and everything he liked especially most
especially a wife to wear the diamonds
each star proof of a miracle see how
the bent fling away their sticks the burning
sweat beads like amber and all bring mangoes
and Fabergé eggs to the healer and yet and yet
it is always the case from long-lip witches
to the court of the Louis that the doctor's love
and the doctor's wife are not the same oh not
even the same species think of Céline
racing through St-Germain-des-Prés shrieking
STOP DYING ALL OF YOU STOP THIS INSTANT
you can't expect these guys to be straight not
these days Dr. does not for the hell of it
cry out loud from his fire red wagon please

11

he can't put on his stereoscope without
he hears the low sea slumber in his soul's
shell spiral not doing well at all is
Dr. tick goes his tinny heart tick
etc will not make it through the why
why is death not 3 tipped stones in a
grassy churchyard why is it this they go
through your milkwhite hands like water
and no toy helps not a whistle not a wheel
and nobody ever gets better not any more
oh when will it ever be Saturday again

THE BEE-EATER

We walk on air, Watson.

—SYLVIA PLATH

FOR CAROL MUSKE

The killer bees—Africanized—have reached San Diego
and I got a C− in Elementary Sci.
New evidence every day that I wasted my youth
on English Lit. That is, I don't know shit
about pollination or why bugs are our friends.
Not that I haven't followed them north
year by year, valley by valley, bearing
the beaded sungod of El Dorado,
the dewdrop gleam of the eagle priests
who heal by sting and pistil. How many times
have I bolted awake with a guilty terror—
the swarm upon me, roaring like a 747.
Once even dreamed I was eating them
like a mouthful of blackberries

                         taste of
gunmetal and caramel

                             couldn't scream
through the foam of pain

                    A veritable
balloon-man all through my tenth summer, I was
the bees' bullseye. The whole hive courted me—
yellowjackets, blue-bellied hornets, furry
bumbles, two-inch wasps. I drew them like
a rotten plum. By August I was on a steroid
drip. Next year they let me be, and the next
and the next, but you never lose the fear
of buzzing

               roses are never the same

                         nor sweets
nor syrup nor even soap. You wash with

oatmeal, chew garlic, dress gray, screen
callers, wander only after dark—

Now I know how an allergy works:
life gives you an A in your own disease.
You take a little venom at a time
and soon you purr with tolerance. Say one
a day, stinger applied directly to the tongue
or sucked like a quivering lozenge.
Self-treatment you'll say is risky:
Jack London OD'd at 40, needling
himself for tropical fevers, and all
the wolves in Yellowknife howled
at the moon in grief
                    but no entomologists

Addiction may occur. Look, the doctors
don't know shit either. The bee-men
got their timetable wrong, and here I am,
not immune enough. If I don't start eating now
they'll be here, covering the house
like a pear tree. Measure my days
by sting if I have to. It's August,
the garden is moaning, we have no
winter to hide in. So bring on the just
desserts, the honey-domed, the dream-
candy kamikaze panacea kiss of death.

Oh bees my bees, come take me.

BUCKLEY

favors castration or failing that a small
tattoo on the upper thigh in the thick-haired
swirl by the balls hot and rank in a Bike
no shower hockeysweat Buckley's upper
lip fairly puckers at the thought or else
a scarlet letter F I guess but cubist
Buckley's in no rush he's breaking bread with
Lady Couldn't-You-Di and sailing to
Byzantium for the weekend moonless nights
he lies on deck and dictaphones the tale
of Bucko Bill countercounterspy and Company
Übermensch Turnbull and Assered to the tits
stoically libidinous if pressed
at tennis a prince and *vingt-et-un* how far
from the terminal wing the suites are ask
the doe-eyed cons in Sing Sing Buckley keeps
in cigs and Nestlés pleading the dago guv
for Clemenceau the traitor every peace
is dirty pink triangles have a nice
retro feel & for quarantine there's islands
off Cape Ann so bare and stony no Brahmin'd
be caught dead in its lee shore a Statue of
Bondage blindfold torch snuffed a whole theme park
of hate monorail geek-dunk Inquisition
daily 10 and 3 heigh-ho mouse-eared dwarfs
in Future Perfect a mushroom cloud like spun
sugar oh Buckley the thing is I agree
about Soviet wheat the Shah the Joint Chiefs
can have all the toilet seats they like but
somehow your pantaloons are in a froth
to cheerlead the dying of my pink people
covered with a condom head to toe St. Paul
of the boneyard guillotining dicks bug-eyed
which reminds me who does the makeup on
Firing Line Frank E. Campbell how did you
get to be such a lady without surgery
I want my F for fag of course on the left
bicep twined with a Navy anchor deck

of Luckies curled in my tee sleeve just the look
to sport through a minefield beating a path
to smithereens arm in arm friend & friend
bivouacked 2 by 2 odd men out so
far out they can almost see over the wall
no more drilling Latin to meatbrain boys
not 50 before they're 30 not skittish
and not going back in Bill no matter how
many cardinals sit on your face oh rest
easy the spit on your grave will pool and mirror
the birdless sky and your children's children
kneel in the waste dump scum of you a popish
rot greening their knees and their Marcos earrings
and spring will maggot the clipped Connecticut
yard of your secret heart ink and bleed me
name and number and I will dance on you

ED DYING

Hate is an old man fucking, arduous
and half a bone, but I work at it
like Sophie Tucker, a last geriatric fling
like pushing a car uphill with a rope.
Hate the Reagans and their facile cancers,
all straight people with lives and my brothers
who flee to the continent having buried
their allotment. This is the rage of the 8th
year, bent out of shape, crazily displaced,
yelling at the queerest people because
the scum politicos of the NIH are out
of reach, funding the end of the world.
I massacre whoever gets in my small way—check
lost in the mail, promise of shirts Friday,
876-4466 my Thrifty druggist rings busy busy
and I need refills like a one-arm bandit,
that kind of thing. As for Ed, Ed is dying
by phone, dwindling in secret, doing without
spunk and visitors. I leave word weekly
on his machine, reports of my latest tantrum,
a recent self-immolation in the Mayfair checkout.
For months there is no reply, but we are
light-years beyond good manners, Ed and I,
loathing bullshit so and the comfort of sunny
disposition. Checked in the day Rita Hayworth died:
Hi Ed, poor Gilda, huh? My only friend who knows
how blonde the lady from Shanghai was and why
it matters so. Publicity errs on the bright side
always, burning for us to have a good time.
Ed who has met them all—Cary, Hitch, Her Serene
Highness—is the last living link between us
poor queens and *To Catch a Thief,* speaking of Eden
lost. Now we are all on the last train out,
fleeing fleeing, diamonds up our ass, the past
curling like smoke as Marlene drags her last
Gitane. Even as Ed is dying, in Washington
everyone eats his boogers and Mormons file
the plague under Pest Control, Reagan's colon

clear as a bagpipe, his sausage tumors
replicated in lifelike vinyl for souvenirs.
Then suddenly over New Year's: *This is Ed.*
Thank you for all your messages. I love
your rage. So I hate mostly for Ed's sake now,
and the old man fucking with his dick in a brace
has mounted a bimbo who can't feel it, does it
for fifty, next year will do it for thirty-five
and eat his shorts for an encore. There are easier
ways than all this slamming about, I admit,
but the time comes—say after the third pneumonia,
and they send you home to recuperate with
the wrong dose, 200 fucking milligrams less
than what will make you live again, and ten
days later you're back in stir, starting it all
over, over and over—the time will come
when you prove you are still alive just feeling
anything at all. So sometimes we are wronged
as Lana Turner in the fifties, jilted and stomped,
herded like misfits, the vanishing years aching
like a torrent of smoke thrown by a moonlit train
bound for the chaos of Shanghai. And if we wail
and spew bile we say we are not collaborators,
for Ed would not be dying please without
the complicity of niceness, so many smiling
colon exams. Yes it's hard to keep it up,
me and this numb member of mine, rutting
while Rome burns, but to hate everything
half-true—including me, especially me—
a nasty temper works like Spanish fly.
Be hard and cry foul, I order my bad thing,
for we are in enemy hands, buying time like
fallen women in countries torn by the death
grip of keeping things polite. Hate for the same
reason a man might sit and weep: missing Ed.

TO GB FROM TUSCANY

Always wondering what's left besides us
and how much time, I stare at the bright
fall of morning on the gray/blue columns
of Santo Spirito, the calm stone of Brunelleschi
washed smooth in a river of mind over matter.
Galileo believed in the opposite of God
for which the penalty was being shut up
with the truth, like cellmates. There is no
gay life in Italy, they all want to go
to New York, not having heard it is
no longer there. I can't tell you how much
you would like today, the pomegranates
heaped in baskets, air drowsy with wood-smoke,
last night a wind down the Arno that set
the moon's teeth on edge. In 1348 the Plague
took a third of Florence, four out of five
in Siena, and there were no baths to close.
Now and then you will see soldiers with nothing
to fight, eating gelato around a Jeep,
and one will look like he just posed
for Michelangelo, who sculpted what he could
not have or be. Or even more naked still,
the courtiers in striped tights and codpieces
strutting in the Piccolomini frescoes, as if
they didn't inhabit an age of blood
that ate young men for breakfast. You'd like
the burnt-siena of the cleared fields,
the pang of yellow shivering through the vines,
scholarly rows of sycamores leading you down
a country road with a promise that nothing ends.
I am not a fan of autumn even so,
but would like to split with you a Tuscan apple
half and half. The light is so clear at four
that every cypress stiffens, honey seeps
in every crevice, no wall escapes the gold
flaunting like a slut. What we seek
from love is depth of field, precisely what
we go to countries for. I brought no camera

19

on this trip, can no more freeze in time
the rosy stone of Assisi than I can
our numbers. Which of the painters of the 1300s
(who can keep them straight) got left behind
in '48? Next time I promise we'll go
together. But I warn you, my friend: in Italy
the men of our tribe live with their widowed
mothers, and the mothers never die. A perfect
circle, that. Monday a black-eyed monk, say 30,
cruised me for half a second in the nave
not 50 feet from where Saint Francis
lies still as a bird with no way south.
Where we are going otherwise I cannot say
beyond November, but these are the shades of marble
a Tuscan hill is capable of: cobalt, ash,
midnight, green ink, tawny, blinding white,
stones fit for a jeweler, towers of them,
streets cobbled with vulcan rock that gleams
like jet in the rain. I miss you of course,
but you know that part. The queer thing is,
Tuscany has already started to be
a dream again, even to me. The last night
I sit at the mouth of the Tiber, on a harbor
shaded by plane trees, eating calamari
fried, and don't know what I am bringing home.
You can have half of whatever it is, once
I change my *lire* back to dollars. Think of
the apple as down payment. In certain
Tuscan places you begin to see how time,
like anything else worth the covering
of autumn ground—us for instance—mines
its gold and shimmer from the deepest field,
even when the days grow short. Such light.

WAITING TO DIE

takes longer now: whole pharmacies of pain
killers and stopgaps, arsenals of slow
motion hand grenades lobbed at the viral
castle. The trickier thing is where to wait:
you pay by the day, no weekly rates in peak
season. Some are wasted at home craning
out the last bedroom window, some in camps
barbed in the high Mojave, very Japanese
in feeling. Some have no idea where.
Nobody waits all day, not every minute,
there's always sleep. Just last August I stopped
in David's garden, heatstruck as a sundial,
woozy with memory overload, forgetting
the late hour. Van Gogh waited in Saint-Rémy
blissed out on a jailyard's flowers, alive
as long as the irises, not dying half
so much as they. Go with the first frost
if possible, miss nothing green. David's place
wide as an island breaks into dogwood,
cherry and wild crab in about ten weeks—
too late now. Whereas spring is already out
of its mind in California, foothills gripped
by sudden pasture, moss on clay, overnight
jasmine clear as a bell. Mid-February
is May here, these narrow weeks of Irish
and months and months of summer coming, pale
as straw and ready to burn. "I look like
E.T.," David drawled, fetching a friend to
supper, careless of shuddering *maître d*'s,
fingers drumming Gershwin. A medicine chest
rides us like a sidecar, like the red-nosed
Fields with his hip flask: *I always carry*
a bottle of snake-oil in my pocket. Carry
the snake too. Spring grows steeper and
steeper, its fifty million irises alone.
Still, there must be something in bloom
somewhere to set on the snow of David's winter
island, being as the roses missed him.

A southern boy learns to play hard to get
before he's out of short pants. So do we
flirt with death, every stem we cut, the riot
of life in a single flower that will not last
the weekend. He never saw Hawaii at all
or anywhere West of East. "Oh you'll love it,"
I raptured, thoughtless in my August swoon.
Once I saw a hardy Boston lady stroke
a pot of ivy above her sink. "Westminster
Abbey," she boasted, who'd smuggled a cutting
through Customs in her purse. Why not that?
A specimen slip from the far edge of aloha,
cliffs for miles vertical green, exploding
orchids down a rotted volcano, rimless
emerald. Its furthest valley is a box
canyon facing the sea, unapproachable
by land. They don't have spring in places
that have no reason. There the leper Koolau
made his stand, him and a band of others
as other as he, who would not go to Molokai
when the great roundup gathered the stooped
and limbless, locking them in waiting rooms.
Angry like us Koolau held his valley
twenty years, the knit of his skin intricate
as a spider tattoo. Something from there would be
nice and gaudy in David's room, whose windows
command the white secret of his garden. A jade
plum sweet as Carolina after rain, borne
ten thousand miles, Venus chasing Mars across
the starry sky. Whatever hurts, whatever
dies at home, bring in flowers as long as
you can, because you are going West
where David is too soon, under this island,
all your waiting done. So go in bloom.

David Almgren
2.14.88
West Island

STEPHEN AT THE FDA

raging under a banner crosslegged
in the intersection spitting at traffic
stop the world if necessary how many T-
cells do you need to yell your head off
Nelson Mandela has less than us and shouts
just lovely peace is hell nobody
gets arrested easy 3 weeks short of
the bad accession of the bush-league
dickhead rimming the black hole of Reagan
keep America nice but nice is over
for our guys so we escalate and Steve
lies down in front of a bus go nowhere
rotten transit not to Dachau Soweto
Township all the white burbs of hate be
homeless today with us the last stand
of genderfuck red-lined X's on our doors
burning Maryland down because we have
nothing to lose queer place admittedly
to be in love but wars ago they did it
in trenches airbursts all around blown
to bits and bloodbrothers still more dear
at the end of the world than ever what is
the last desire
                    to be known
                              the last
passion the wish to awaken bright
as the gold October sun grazing the slow
shivering fields of what remains we keep
this day for the fallen all their names
are the stone that people who live in glass
houses fear a hole in the south basement
no turning back and the L.A. 6
pour in Steve at the rear rioting
through the cubicles of death marauding
FREE THE DRUGS as if a cure had ever
paid the rent vote Republican Dan
Quayle for Himmler expect no release
the oldest prison is what the hets

do to our hearts with hate jailing us
in solitary please I admit I'm here
because I love Steve as much as freedom
fuck I hope that's not politically in-
correct pigs with clubs pour in after
like Keystone Kops oh Stephen don't resist
don't piss them off finally he's dragged out
cuffed and pale and loud HELP US WE'RE
DYING more man than I today but hey
we're easy I'll be a man tomorrow
and last night we both were they board
him on the bus and I touch the window
how do you stop time same way you stop
evil by refusing to go we are the thing
they fear the most Stevie more than plague
more than the dungeon houses they home to
every night they fear us out we leave
the system in smithereens bureaucrats
standing appalled on the upper floors unable
to commute and tonight we will lie in
the Shenandoah twined in each other
above the blood ground of the rebel army
thrown away on the wrong cause but did they
kiss did they squander were they men
at last like us at the bottom of time
make noise my guerrilla my love stay
on fire we will bring down nations

LOVE ALONE
18 ELEGIES FOR ROG

(1988)

Love can not fill the thickened lung with breath,
Nor clean the blood, nor set the fractured bone;
Yet many a man is making friends with death
Even as I speak, for lack of love alone.

—EDNA ST. VINCENT MILLAY

PREFACE

Above all I am not concerned with poetry.
My subject is War, and the pity of War.
The poetry is in the pity.

—WILFRED OWEN, 1918

Wilfred Owen's *Preface* to the poems he wrote in 1917 and 1918 is the best caution I know against beauty and eloquence. He begs us not to read his anthem for the doomed youth of his generation as a decorous celebration of heroes. Decorum is the contemptible pose of the politicians and preachers, the hypocrite slime whose grinning hatred slicks this dying land like rotten morning dew. I do not presume on the nightmare of Owen's war—may the boys of Flanders be spared all comparison—and I don't pretend to have written the anthem of my people. But I would rather have this volume filed under AIDS than under Poetry, because if these words speak to anyone they are for those who are mad with loss, to let them know they are not alone.

Roger Horwitz, my beloved friend, died on 22 October 1986, after nineteen months of fighting the ravages of AIDS. He was forty-four years old, the happiest man I ever knew. He fought with an immensity of spirit that transfigured us who loved him. On his grave are Plato's last words on Socrates: *the wisest and justest and best*. Rog had a constitutional aversion to bullshit and was incapable of being unkind. Though he held two degrees from Harvard—a Ph.D. in Comparative Literature and a law degree—he made no show of it. The only thing he ever bragged about were his three bohemian years in Paris in his early twenties, and he didn't so much boast of them as endlessly give them away.

These elegies were written during the five months after he died, one right after the other, with hardly a half day's pause between. Writing them quite literally kept me alive, for the only time I wasn't wailing and trembling was when I was hammering at these poems. I have let them stand as raw as they came. But because several friends have wished for a few commas or a stanza break here and there, I feel I should make a comment on their form. I don't mean them to be impregnable, though I admit I want them to allow no escape, like a hospital room, or indeed a mortal illness.

In the summer of 1984 Roger and I were in Greece together, and for both of us it was a peak experience that left us dazed and slightly giddy. We'd been together for ten years, and life was very sweet. On the high bluff of ancient Thera, looking out across the southern Aegean toward Africa, my hand grazed a white marble block covered edge to edge with Greek characters, line after precise line. The marble was tilted face up to the weather, its message slowly eroding in the rain. "I hope somebody's recorded all this," I said, realizing with a dull thrill of helplessness that this *was* the record, right here on this stone.

When I began to write about AIDS during Roger's illness, I wanted a form that would move with breathless speed, so I could scream if I wanted and rattle on and empty my Uzi into the air. The marbles of Greece kept coming back to mind. By the time Roger died the form was set—not quite marble, not quite Greek—but it was in my head that if only a fragment remained in the future, to fade in the sulfurous rain, it would say how much I loved him and how terrible was the calamity.

The story that endlessly eludes the decorum of the press is the death of a generation of gay men. What is written here is only one man's passing and one man's cry, a warrior burying a warrior. May it fuel the fire of those on the front lines who mean to prevail, and of their friends who stand in the fire with them. We will not be bowed down or erased by this. I learned too well what it means to be a people, learned in the joy of

my best friend what all the meaningless pain and hor-
ror cannot take away—that all there is is love. Pity us
not.

Los Angeles
29 June 1987

HERE

everything extraneous has burned away
this is how burning feels in the fall
of the final year not like leaves in a blue
October but as if the skin were a paper lantern
full of trapped moths beating their fired wings
and yet I can lie on this hill just above you
a foot beside where I will lie myself
soon soon and for all the wrack and blubber
feel still how we were warriors when the
merest morning sun in the garden was a
kingdom after Room 1010 war is not all
death it turns out war is what little
thing you hold on to refugeed and far from home
oh sweetie will you please forgive me this
that every time I opened a box of anything
Glad Bags One-A-Days KINGSIZE was
the worst I'd think will you still be here
when the box is empty Rog Rog who will
play boy with me now that I bucket with tears
through it all when I'd cling beside you sobbing
you'd shrug it off with the quietest *I'm still*
here I have your watch in the top drawer
which I don't dare wear yet help me please
the boxes grocery home day after day
the junk that keeps men spotless but it doesn't
matter now how long they last or I
the day has taken you with it and all
there is now is burning dark the only green
is up by the grave and this little thing
of telling the hill I'm here oh I'm here

GARDENIAS

pain is not a flower pain is a root
and its work is underground where the moldering
proceeds the bones of all our joy winded
and rained and nothing grows a whole life's love
that longed to be an orchard forced to lie
like an onion secret sour in the mine of pain
the ore veined out there's just these tunnels shot
with roots but then we were never gardeners
were we planters waterers cleanup crew
more yard boys three bucks an hour than rose queens
still the place was the vale of Arcady to us
and after all a man can plant a stone here
and it'll sprout but gardenias now those vellum
Billie Holiday prom flowers what a shock
to learn they grew on *trees* well bushes then
we urned one in the shade of the Chinese elm
watered and watered the white blooms wafting May
to mid-August now and then you'd bring one in
floating in a bowl and leave it on my desk
by such small tokens did the world grow green
and the Billie Holiday song is this I'm jealous
of all the time I didn't know you yet
and the month since so full of risible scalding
blankness I crave it more that secondhand past
oh you can keep the lovers the far countries
but you young you twenty you in Paris
with a poem in your boot if I could have that
really be there then beside you or waving
across Boulevard St-Germain I'd face these
dead days longer the cave of all that's left
enough now as to gardenias look this is
such a cliché but one happened to break
in October by then I was bringing them in
leaving them at your bedside between the Kleenex
and the talking clock *Smell it good now Rog*
it's the last one fourth day yellow and smutty
yet I gave you one last whiff right under
your nose while you talked to Jaimee then

you died a week later and that next day
I was out in the garden to die of the pain
but wait what is this Thomas Hardy a furled
gardenia just coming out which I bowled by
the bed I sleep now just where you slept curled
in the selfsame spot and that one lasted through
the funeral next week and a third billowed out
what is this *Twilight Zone* which I laid on
the grave as if I was your date for the prom
which I would've been if we'd ever been 18
but for all the spunk of the three gardenias
still the pain is not a flower and digs like
a spade in stony soil no earthly reason
not a thing will come of it but a slag heap
and a pit and the deepest root the stuff of witch
banes winds and winds its tendril about my heart
I promise you all the last gardenias Rog
but they can't go on like this they've stopped they know
the only garden we'll ever be is us and it's
all winter they tried they tried but oh the ice
of my empty arms my poor potato dreams

THE WORRYING

ate me alive day and night these land mines
all over like the toy bombs dropped on the
Afghans little Bozo jack-in-the-boxes
that blow your hands off 3 A.M. I'd go
around the house with a rag of ammonia
wiping wiping crazed as a housewife on *Let's
Make a Deal* the deal being PLEASE DON'T MAKE
HIM SICK AGAIN faucets doorknobs the phone
every lethal thing a person grips and leaves
his prints on scrubbed my hands till my fingers
cracked washed apples ten times ten no salad but
iceberg and shuck the outer two thirds someone
we knew was brain dead from sushi so stick
to meatloaf creamed corn spuds whatever we
could cook to death DO NOT USE THE D WORD
EVEN IN JEST when you started craving deli
I heaved a sigh because salami was so de-
germed with its lovely nitrites to hell with
cholesterol that's for people way way over
the hill or up the hill not us in the vale
of borrowed time yet I was so far more gone
than you nuts in fact ruinous as a supermom
with a kid in a bubble who can't play and ten
years later can't work can't kiss can't laugh
but his room's still clean every cough every
bump would nothing ever be nothing again
cramming you with zinc and Häagen-Dazs so wild
to fatten you up I couldn't keep track of
what was medicine what old wives' but see
THERE WAS NO MEDICINE only me and to
circle the wagons and island the last of our
magic spoon by spoon nap by nap till we
healed you as April heals drinking the sun
I was Prospero of the spell of day-by-day
and all of this just the house worry peanuts
to what's out there and you with the dagger at

your jugular struggling back to work jotting
your calendar two months ahead penciling
clients husbanding husbanding inching back
and me agape with the day's demises who
was swollen who gone mad ringing you on
the hour how are you compared to ten noon
one come home and have blintzes petrified
you'd step in an elevator with some hacking
CPA the whole world ought to be masked
please I can't even speak of the hospital fear
fists bone white the first day of an assault
huddled by your bed like an old crone empty-
eyed in a Greek square black on black the waiting
for tests the chamber of horrors in my head
my rags and vitamins dumb as leeches how did
the meningitis get in where did I slip up
what didn't I scour I'd have swathed the city
in gauze to cushion you no man who hasn't
watched his cruelest worry come true in a room
with no door can ever know what doesn't
die because they lie who say it's over
Rog it hasn't stopped at all are you okay
does it hurt what can I do still still I
think if I worry enough I'll keep you near
the night before Thanksgiving I had this
panic to buy the plot on either side of us
so we won't be cramped that yard of extra grass
would let us breathe THIS IS CRAZY RIGHT but
Thanksgiving morning I went the grave two over
beside you was six feet deep ready for the next
murdered dream so see the threat was real
why not worry worry is like prayer is like
God if you have none they all forget there's
the other side too twelve years and not once
to fret WHO WILL EVER LOVE ME that was
the heaven at the back of time but we had it
here now black on black I wander frantic
never done with worrying but it's mine it's
a cure that's not in the books are you easy

my stolen pal what do you need is it
sleep like sleep you want a pillow a cool
drink oh my one safe place there must be
something just say what it is and it's yours

NEW YEAR'S AT LAWRENCE'S GRAVE

What splendour! Only the tawny eagle
could really sail out into the splendour of it all.

—D. H. LAWRENCE

FOR BETTY SENESCU

Santa Fe was awful but don't go by me
I was just trying to get *here* the turquoise
boutique rug hunger gave me the bends fast
the strut of the Malibu skiers the bleach desert
not north enough not high enough I wanted
my nose to bleed the powder dry of blue snow
to frost and crack my hands up State 68
rippling beside the Rio Grande scarce wide
enough for a proper river no melt yet
so why the rush thus tamely you rise up to
the Taos plain the shock so sudden you jettison
your booster stage without even thinking WAIT
aloft in pure space and the higher you climb
toward Lawrence the savage alluvial moon
of Jupiter on your left stretches to Arizona
the sacred mountains wall the east piñon-crowded
snow-slashed older than we can dream now take
the last dirt track to Kiowa eagle land
for sure rutting to Frieda's ranch bought for
a song specific the autograph MS of *Sons*
and Lovers fair-traded to Mrs. Dodge
three rude cabins on a piney knoll pasture
below where Susan the cow switched flies all
plain as a clod of earth the drop-jaw view
millennial remorseless if that is your
sort of beauty then here is where to come
preferably with a spot on the lung and Pan's
pipe for a pen the final climb on foot
switchbacks the white hill the chapel up top
snug as a woodshed *chapel's* wrong *shrine* oh
please *place* is all you need but not as in

final resting nothing could be further
off a stucco eagle caps the roofpeak
unless it's a phoenix the window in the eave's
the pinwheel hub of a tractor tire unglazed
inside was yellow once faded as Assisi
the altar cask silver-paint with DHL
incised a half-inch deep just above in a
shallow niche a second eagle neck cracked
east window a daisy-streaked wagon wheel
lowly offerings everywhere pine cones rock
chips acorns a single long-dead rose like the
windfall of tempests a glacier's lavish spoor
from us Rog I left the first day a double
sprig of evergreen next morning two downed
oak leaves parchment brown and flawless gathered
them off the hill like a deer and prayed open-eyed
Lorenzo teach me fire let me go out
burning he was your age Rog sang himself
to sleep like a canary in a coal mine
and the twist of fate versus him and Frieda
and you and me is the writer got left behind
in our case also not such a great canary
in blue snowlight at this year's close I sobbed
and sobbed for us all the New Year's deadborn
way up here the date that counts is the one
that follows the hyphen as our one sere day
is 10/22 Lorenzo went in April
five months shy of forty-five and you
just thirty days I'm so rapacious of time
I hoard the extra four months as if they
weren't like everything else blown away in
the first good wind I wander graveyards now
like a math quiz figuring who we've beaten
I came to Lawrence for having about the same
to prove a man can leave the world burned clean
at forty-four and then the long climb down
the sun's rim the bare lace branches of the
cottonwoods like a line of Indian dancers
at the brink of every stream the horses in ones
and twos in meadows so wide you can see

the curve of the planet all the vastness Lawrence
never got enough of why is it given
to me whose soul is smashed to bits such doused
and dwindled fire a man who could write about
anything and the god in it would seethe
and drool with lust where is the phoenix now
now is the day of his rising or we are
all dead driving back to Taos I hung
a right and crossed the moon to the gorge bridge
maybe thirty miles upriver from the last
look remember how un-Grande it seemed well
here it was a river of flame in a rift
in Jupiter seven hundred feet below
a ribbon of jade and whitecap everything takes
forever and not one man with a spare minute
so bereft is the old year Rog your bullet
in its heart *Perhaps if I came back to New
Mexico I would get up again* says Lawrence
dying in Vence and see how he came back
just ashes years are born without him still
years don't care how rifted time has grown they
thrive on ashes pity this tremendous sky
this thundering country its goat-god is gone
long may its endless distance gray and ochre
ease his native spirit if only you
were here Rog it's the sort of beauty we
always walked in arm in arm we'd read him
out loud and bring him back I can't alone
the ashes of too much grief have choked the song
of mountains in me there are men who still
belong here oh eagle-flame of Taos
why have you wasted your splendor on me

MANIFESTO

unsolicited Adam S diagnosed 9/85
and lucky calls to say all sickness is self-
induced and as I start to growl oozes self-
beatification *taking a course in miracles*
he says and I bark my way out of his wee
kirk and savage his name from the Rolodex
another triumph of self-love like metaphysical
sit-ups a washboard ripple on the pre-
frontal lobe doubtless the work of Mrs. Hay
baghwan of the leper set Pooh-bear in hand
purveying love-is-you with an anchorlady's
do and Diane Arbus eyes straight-faced told
a reporter people in train wrecks bring it on
themselves *But what if somebody gets the virus*
from a transfusion WHAT ARE THEY DOING NEEDING
BLOOD IN THE FIRST PLACE pounces Lady Hay
every sucker in the ICU's to blame see
there are no microbes just self-loathing come
sit in a ring with St. Louise and deep-throat
your pale sore body lick your life like a dog's
balls and repeat after me I AM A MIRACLE
why do I care about all this who does it
harm shouldn't the scared and solo have a shot
at warding it off six months a year by dint
of mellowness well yes and no we need
the living alive to bucket Ronnie's House
with abattoirs of blood hand in hand lesions
across America need to trainwreck the whole
show till someone listens so no they may not
coo in mirrors disbarring the fevered the choked
and wasting as losers who have not learned
like Adam the yoga with which to kiss their own
asshole every tent revival mantra
is one less bomb tossed in the red-taped labs
of the FDA one less bureaucrat pelted
as he chews his Pilate's thumb toddling home
by limo to Silver Springs where all high-risk
behavior is curfewed after dusk forget it

the boys at Mrs. Hay's haven't an anarchist
bone in their spotted torsos miraculized
they may be but even if they last forever
will only love the one poor thing themself
and bury the rest of us spring in their stride
as they whistle home with the shovel thinking
I'm still here the level earth wide as they
can see strewn with burn and ruin like a
crash site but I admit it I love you better
than me Rog always have you're no different
all the migrainous interchange with crooks
and fools lines at the post that inch like Poland
dogged nerves of a day's wage how much self
is functional by Thursday afternoon unless
it has a weekend place remote as Na Pali
green as the light on Daisy's dock the boys
of Hay are learning how to laugh again
but what if one never forgot in the first
place oh boys I warn you now joy alone
will not protect you have it all you can
lie if you have to say you believe in
Oral Roberts's eighty-foot Jesus with
the ransom note but keep your miracles small
my friend and I we laughed for years on end
and the dark fell anyway and all our people
sicken and have no rage the Feds are lying
about the numbers the money goes for toilet
seats in bombers the State of the Union
is pious as Pius washing his hands of Hitler
Jews are not a Catholic charity when is
enough enough I had a self myself
once but he died when do we leave the mirror
and lie down in front of the tanks let them
put two million of us away see how quick
it looks like Belsen force out all their hate
the cool indifferent genocide that locks up
all the pills whatever it takes witness
the night and the waste for those who are not yet
touched for soon the thing will ravish their women

their jock sons lie in rows in the empty infield
the scream in the streets will rise to a siren din
and they will beg us to teach them how to
bear it we who are losing our reason

THE HOUSE ON KINGS ROAD

*Raphael, your verses should be written so
that they will have . . . something in them of our life,
so that the rhythm and each phrase will show
that an Alexandrian is writing of an Alexandrian.*

—C. P. CAVAFY

they will take me out feet first the orphan house
may not even notice right off for houses
are slow and set in their ways probably not
till the FOR SALE sign is stabbed by the front steps
will it groan in its sleep not till the movers
locust through bundling tagging the odd lot
of our mute remains will its Yale locks seize
like clotting blood desperate to keep us home
but as for now it's our last stand the halfway
house we thought to rest in going up except
the way is vertigo down the summit was just
a view of Fuji never meant to be scaled
only to gaze on far when houses fall
in Sophocles the blood of a king's name
is sown with salt downstage is hip-deep in
courtiers the princesses are led away
from ballet class to do their last lift for
a firing squad but what happens to people's
rooms the chair just so to catch the morning
the drawer of pennies the unmade bed aswirl
with the night's turning does anything manage to
memorize the place before it's trucked off
or is nobody's room permitted the smallest pause
unless a spinster's left to keep it in amber
a few years more but the auctioneer can wait
the quill on Dickens's desk is exactly where
he laid it everyone else is a slippery tenant
who can blame a house for being leery
always left in the lurch gas off phone cut
whatever time remains let the brief museum
of Kings Road be all mine I am the Board

of Trustees I am the Hoving I decide
what's out what's in vaults and I alone will
know the hours prepared to shutter like Paris
on the merest whim Starlite Tours idles
below at Chevy Chase's then up at the top
by Steve Martin apparently we are a highly
comic canyon our pedigree rich as Rue
de Fleurus Bacall and Bogie in living noir
champagning away the forties at 1600
Here's looking at you kid eight-forty-one
a month seemed an act of madness till it
stubbornly never went up like rent imagine
an IRS deduction for finding safe harbor
for the heart life's a roof my gentle housemate
lost at the front door still I bawl *I'm home Rog*
not that I really expect to meet you pouring
a glass of milk but the layout here is pregnant
as a stage mad to get in on the act *As You
Like It* poolside *Lear* in the back bedroom
and me the perfect audience all applause
fixed roof your diary scrawls *skimmed pool pasta
for supper* stuff you wouldn't suppose worth
the ink yet somehow it breaches the wall
within the wall more than memory more than
the pivot of event calls us home shoring
time with casual embraces unremarkable
as sky no set like Juliet's balcony
no histrionics star turns curtain calls
just the putting a house in order most
gay men live a bare half hour a day middle
of noplace airshaft rooms stacked with *Playbills*
socks balled tight as summer camp picking up
after themselves as if they keep a spare
mom in the closet up and down the city
the CEOs with the bearded ladies the pencil-
thin monsignors in Scarlett drag bachelors
live in bachelor flats can always be counted
to square a table need no china of their own
or knives inhabit their charm like tortoises
the landlady sweeps them clean in a day if they

43

chance to die but they die in a little hole
offstage so dinner is not delayed in small
towns they never leave home at all but sleep
in footed flannel pajamas merit badges
pinned in a row on the chest of drawers begging
the question wouldn't you think anywhere
would be a move up refrigerator crate
under 101 heating vent Eighth and Olive
up a fucking tree you have to crave your own
room before all else track it hammer it
steal it life may deal you a snowy doorway
leave you a gypsy lose your shoes and John
Doe tagged to your ankle but the dream house
is worth it it got you somewhere die in
its shady yard bougainvillea rippling
like a coral reef gold on the west windows
or only reach the lookout stare at the house
impossible on the far hill well at least
it's there it exists depart in peace your sigh
will merge with the mountain's echo beckoning
some just out of high school some in the army
one by one they set out in a terror of hope
visioning the place and the friend with a key
its threshold level with life as the cabin
on Walden world enough and nine tall trees
it's our house Rog I've got all the papers
so what if the legalese says *single man*
and *single man* beside our separate names
the law lies like the church lies the elders
cane their moonstruck sons and play at castles
Writing may be either the record of a deed
or a deed Thoreau says okay just this once may
this be a deed lawyerproof filed at the hall
of records that two men ceased to be single
here in a house free of liens and the rule
of sorry kings and sometimes would look up
from a book from peeling an apple their bright
astonished eyes would meet and nearly falter
gladness is like looking at the sun how can
Death untwine them or the room in the room

where they have one name oh my love tell me
where you are in the study writing Follain
laughing on the phone a bowl of pistachios
shucked beside you standing in the courtyard
shears in hand like a dousing rod surveying
the shape of an hour's pruning well then we both
must be taking a nap curled like spoons on
a rainy Sunday terror and evil banished
like the snakes in Ireland even fast asleep
you know you are holding the key and you must
keep it in trust for the children of children
who want you dead and maybe the timidest son
will know his name find his burning friend and come
unlock the dream a month before you went
you cried *What happened to our happy life*
staring blind out over the garden Rog
it's here it's here I know because I am
the ghost who haunts us I am the last window
sir tread lightly who bargain for this house
you are sporting with kings on a high road
despite the sifted gray of time where things
are atomized the white chairs under the elm
the wall of books laid brick by brick the lamp
pooling on the blue-bound Plato as we held
our ground through August let the material go
what you cannot buy or have in your name
is the ghost of a touch the glancing stroke
as a man passes through a room where his love
sits reading later much later the nodding head
of the one on the other's shoulder no title
usurps that place this is its home forever

BROTHER OF THE MOUNT OF OLIVES

Mine, O thou lord of life, send my roots rain.

—Gerard Manley Hopkins

combing the attic for anything extra
missed or missing evidence of us I sift
your oldest letters on onionskin soft-
cover Gallimard novels from graduate school
brown at the edges like pound cake and turn up
an undeveloped film race it to SUNSET
PLAZA ONE-HOUR wait out the hour wacko
as a spy smuggling a chip that might decode
World War III then sit on the curb poring over
prints of Christmas '83 till I hit paydirt
three shots of the hermit abbey on the moors
southeast of Siena our final crisscross
of the Tuscan hills before the sack of Rome
unplanned it was just that we couldn't bear
to leave the region quite the Green Guide barely
gave it a nod *minor Renaissance pile*
but the real thing monks in Benedictine white
pressing olives and gliding about in hooded
silence Benedict having commanded *shh*
along with his gaunt motto *ora et labora*
pray work but our particular brother John
couldn't stop chattering not from the moment
he met us grinning at the cloister door
seventy years olive-cheeked bald and guileless
no matter we spoke no Italian he led us
gesturing left and right at peeling frescoes
porcelain Marys a limpid row of arches
across the court like a trill on a harpsichord
little did he know how up to our eyeballs
we were on the glories of Florence the Bach
geometry of the hill towns their heart-
stopping squares with the well in the middle
and a rampant lion on the governor's roof
we'd already scrutinized every *thing* and now

before we left wished to see it peopled
going about their business out of time
keeping bees holy offices raisin bread
as if nothing had happened since Galileo
instead this voluble little monk pulling us
into the abbey church its lofty Gothic vault
overlaid in sugared Baroque plaster like a bad
cake then Brother John grips us by the biceps
and sweeps us down the cypress-paneled choir
to the reading desk where the Gutenberg
is propped on feast-days he crouches and points
to the inlay on the base and there is a cat
tail curled seeming to sit in a window
every tiger stripe of him laid in jigsaw
as we laughed our rapturous guide went *mew mew*
like a five-year-old *How long have you been here*
we ask a question requiring all our hands
fifty years he tosses off as if time had
nothing to do with it one hand lingering
on my shoulder is it books we like then come
and we patter round the cloister in his wake
duck through a door up a stone stairs and peer
through a grill wrought like a curtain of ivy
into the library its great vellum folios
solid as tombstones nobody copying out
or illuminating today unless perhaps
all of that has died and there's a Xerox
glowing green in the abbot's study John
pokes you to look at the door carvings it seems
he is not a bookish man but who has time
to read any more we must descend and see
the frescoes fifty years without the world
pray work pray work and yet such drunken gaiety
gasping anew at the cloister's painted wall
clutching my hand before the bare-clad Jesus
bound at the pillar by the painter so-called
Sodoma the parted lips the love-glazed eyes
JUST WHAT KIND OF MEN ARE WE TALKING ABOUT
are we the heirs of them or they our secret
fathers and how many of our kind lie beneath

the cypress alley crowning the hill beyond
the bell tower how does one ask such things
with just one's hands then we took three pictures
me and John John and you you and me *click*
as the old monk takes my arm I'm certain now
that he likes touching us that we are a world
inside him whether he knows or not not that
I felt molested I can take care of myself
but a blind and ancient hunger not unspeakable
unsayable you think he knew about us Rog
how could he not pick up the intersect
the way we laughed the glint in our eyes as we
played our Italian for four hands but my sole
evidence is this sudden noon photograph
the two of us arm in arm in the cloister
delirious gold November light of Tuscany
washing our *cinquecento* faces splashing
the wall behind us a fresco of the monks
at dinner high above them in a pulpit
a reader trilling in Latin you can't even
eat without *ora et labora* and we look
squinting at John as if to wonder how
he will ever click the shutter right it's like
giving a watch to a savage but we look
quite wonderful you with the Green Guide me
clutching the pouch with the passports we look
unbelievably young our half smiles precisely
the same for that is the pierce of beauty
that first day of a rose barely started
and yet all there and Brother John so geeky
with the Canon A-1 did he even see what
he caught we look like choirboys or postulants
or a vagabond pair of scholars here to
pore over an undecoded text not religious
but brotherly enough it's a courtly age
where men are what they do and where they go
comrades all we look like no one else Rog
here's the proof in color now the tour is over
we are glided into a vestibule where cards
slide rosaries prayers that tick are gauntly

presided over by a monk senior to John
if not in years then officialdom the air
is strict in here we cut our laughter short
this one's got us pegged right off this keeper
of the canonical cash drawer withering John
with a look that can hardly wait to assign vast
and pointless rosaries of contrition we buy
the stark official guide to Monte Oliveto
leave a puddle of lire *per restauro*
for restorations and then we're free of His
Priestliness and John bundles us off still
merry and irrepressible too old perhaps
to fear the scorn and penitence of those
racked by sins of the flesh who never touch
a thing and ushers us out to the Fiat
bidding us safe journey who's never been
airborne or out to sea or where Shiva
dances or Pele the fire-god gargles
the bowels of the earth we wave him off
and leap in the car we're late for Rome flap
open the map but we're laughing too *Did that
just happen or what* and we drive away
winding up past the tower towards the grove
of graves where the tips of the cypress lean
in the breeze and a hooded monk is walking
head bent over his book of hours in passing
I see that it's John wave and grin *rividerci*
startled at his gauntness fixed on his text dark
his reverie no acknowledgment goodbye
that is the whole story you know about Rome
and flying tourist opening weeks of mail
putting a journey to bed and on and on
but I've thought of John ever since whenever
the smiling Pope makes another of his sub-
human attitudes the law he drives our people
from the temples and spits on the graves of his
brother priests who are coughing to death in cells
without unction and boots the Jesuit shrink
who calls all love holy he wants his fags
quiet *shh* and I try to think of John

and the picture he saved three years for me
till the lost roll of Tuscany came to light
and turned out to hold our wedding portrait
the innocent are so brief and the rigid world
doesn't marry its pagans any more but John
didn't care what nothing we professed he joined
us to join him a ritual not in the book
but his secret heart it doesn't get easier Rog
even now the night jasmine is pouring
its white delirium in the dark and I
will not have it if you can't I shut all
windows still it seeps in with the gaudy
oath of spring oh help be somewhere near
so I can endure this drunk intrusion
of promise where is the walled place where we
can walk untouched or must I be content
with a wedding I almost didn't witness
the evidence all but lost no oath no ring
but the truth sealed to hold against the hate
of the first straight Pope since the Syllabus of
Errors this Polack joke who fears his women
and men too full of laughter far brother
if you should pass beneath our cypresses
you who are a praying man your god can
go to hell but since you are so inclined
pray that my friend and I be still together
just like this at the Mount of Olives blessed
by the last of an ancient race who loved
youth and laughter and beautiful things so much
they couldn't stop singing and we were the song

No Witnesses

(1981)

To Sandy McClatchy and Alfred Corn

My Shirts

To Roger

The first was in a window and was silk,
a chemical green. A deep, thin salesman loved
the hang of it, I think, because it lay
by a shoe and an ounce of scent, open
at the throat, and lent a certain air to this
and that. It was, he wanted you to know,
a look that looked ahead, a dream, but not
for everyone. Eighty dollars a week,
his own cut of the pie, wouldn't touch it.

I wore it for an hour and a half. A ride
on a trolley, swinging by a strap. A shot
of Campari in cream, this in a low-life bar,
like cactus liquor on the tongue, the taste
of dread. I kept the glass against my chest,
a rose on a clover ground. And by and by
(but well within the hour), dispensing with
hellos, I fell in bed, the shirt all shucked
like any other skin.
                          The second was,
well, innocent. Tan and wash-and-wear
and went with what you will, none of your swank
and Spanish dancer overtones. Collar
buttons. It was left, as of little worth,
when my friend went to China, where he died.
When he died, Death altered it, but at first
it fit the house I had as well as his,
and so I brought it home. In time it came
to lie in a ball, the day's last apparel, retrieved
at dusk (the stroke of nerves) and shaken out
and slipped on, oh, until I slept.
                          A bad
habit, since it insisted, like the woodsman's
violin in the old story, on taking

the place of things. At the edge of the wood, the bag
of seed, the hatchet and saw fall. The burden
of the tale is local color and German elves.
Sublime, but nothing to do with life. He plays
a piece evocative of autumn light
shaven to edges across the meadow grass,
a light that swipes at the outer leaves but goes
deeper, rifling limb and trunk and root. What
becomes of his cord of oak? Put in its place.
His cut and dried arrangement lives apart.
His violin, see, has bought the night for a song.

One never bewares enough. In the mirror,
with so much to attend to, one doesn't
take the care one ought about the old fool
in old clothes one is turning into, the cheap
effects of the too long loved. What is really
second nature is not the rumpled shirt
thrown about the shoulders of an evening.
No. One seeks the most comfortable way
to carry Death around, to break him in
and thus to wear him out.
                                        The third would be,
I swore, my safest yet because I knew
what to watch for—and, too, the risk I ran
that what I would have at the end of the week
was a week's wash. Mostly, a dandy learns
the cost of keeping clean the wrong way round.
His drawers are all in disarray. A shirt
is right for breakfast; then, as lunch comes on,
it seems a shame. Only the droll endure.

Cured of making much of whole cloth, I worked
at random on a patchwork. If I saw
the red was dominant, deliberately
I went to green or brown. No inch of it
led anywhere, lacking the thread. A shirt
without tears, whose surface phenomena
are lovely, like the drift of certain snows,
going on and on until they lead you

to believe they never stop sleeping it off.
And so you hurry home to the fire, the snow
goes to water, and you wake to wonder what
you saw. A shirt, in other words, that seems
guileless. *Is* so, if you stick to surfaces.
Underneath, do not forget, the body
is always sorry for one breach or another,
bareback, prey to gooseflesh.

                                  The scraps gave out
in the right sleeve. Remnants I had put by
for years—torn pockets, cuffs the dog brought in
in his teeth, my patches, hems—didn't suffice
or go so far. Far being where the years
had taken *me*, it was a natural
mistake. If time were scraps, I could have plaited
a tent.

          Is this the stuff you want, my love?
My shirts? In a better world, the lovers give
résumés (they have them all typed), a list
of needs, the year that each emerged, and then
the corresponding loss of nerve. In black
and white, all the poop on masks. For instance,
my first arrest involved the theft of a pair
of mesh pajamas. Now I sleep stripped. How
does one explain such reversals? Say this:
that we are sealed to a mirror and more.
More, we care so for the holding still, we don't
get the joke: its silver and ourselves are
only polish.

              Oh, I know I promised
to fit you with beginning, middle, end.
You would be rags if you went out like *this*,
I know. But wear it now. Tonight is what
we have come for. Tomorrow, when we must
be spiffy once again, something suitable
will turn up, starched and ironed, the one shirt
to which we roll our eyes when we cry "Keep
your *shirt* on" or, in pain, "I lost my *shirt*."

Well, we will see about that tomorrow.

Bones and Jewels

TO SANFORD FRIEDMAN

Time has simply got to shut up. Or else
I'll beat him senseless, bind his hands, and saucer
his fat bachelor's face like a discus
on the wind. Then let him try to talk of me
as if I had manners and must make do.
Morbid broken boy, to favor those in pain,
turn me twenty-nine without a wrestle
if you can, so long accustomed to tired
women. I have decided to fight you
early—

        because, one, I am on vacation.
Two, I can use my nails, not much given,
in war at least, to honor yet (and yet
I long for forms, for formulas, I mean—
I can't marry now, my darling x. Why,
I can't thread a needle, and my mother
signed me away at birth to z, who is
in oil. My promises, such as they are
are not my own). And three, why I hate you,
you remind me of the men in Maine.

                Of all

the coasts the sea is heir to, this, this tongue
of Massachusetts, will be taken first—
not, it seems, for several hundred years,
but soon enough. The locals, if they care,
lack the captain's impulse either to sink
with the ship or, like Noah, to pick and choose.
One day, I expect, they will notice how
the high tide seeps among the lilacs (When
did we lose the garden? Wasn't there once
a field as well? And further back, did we,
or am I dreaming, didn't we live high
in the dunes?), and then they will leave the table,
the lobsters cracked and hardly touched, out, down
to the bay to row to Boston.
                              Things to do.
Research before September first the death
of grasses. This far south, when does the brown
come in? Write to Bunny (oh, but lightly).
Ask the Sunday hunter on Ryder downs
why he won't wear red. What is he after?
Stop retrieving shells. The men with buckets,
the tide, the birds won't leave them be. All right,
you leave them be.
                    "Bunny dear, I know you
hate me for a fishwife. I've run away,
where you would lose your temper, have a gin
and lemons, then undertake to reassess
Melville and the whale. The Baptist minister
in town (call him Ishmael) says he won't
dispute the bits of seascape in the Bible.
If they swore that Jonah ate the whale whole,
it is all one to him. Come to Truro,
Bunny (or not! or not!). You are always
in the heart of
                Edna (St. Vicious) Millay."

Fog again. And written down again. Why
bother? Clearly a writer keeps his sad
diary current on ghostly afternoons,
and only then to avert the dark fingers

from the throat. Meteorologically,
assume the worst unless otherwise stated,
as in passages given to paradox,
the notes for a life lived on the loose—

                                     "Sunny.
From bed"—abrupt, in the New York style—"I watch
Achilles dress. I take my Baudelaire
from under the pillow, play at reading it,
and then write in the flyleaf how he is
something less than Achilles in a tie.
He watches me. He thinks I am doing
a poem, as one does, um, one's knitting
or one's horoscope. We'd kill each other
for a price. Unless we got paid, we wouldn't
trouble to pull a trigger and soil the rug—"

Long since, the bitch with the books and time to burn
has come to the end of America. The heat
she heaps on boys, on warriors and thugs,
belies who is it loves *her* least. She's not
a girl in a story, though the story goes
that she was once so pale, a candle passed
in front of her still lit the room beyond,
no matter how she held it, shook it, blew
and spit at it. Here, pen in hand, she walks
the brink, not in a shawl at the lip of a cliff,
but further than is safe. To tell the truth,
the seas with any drama are confined
to Maine—the undertow, the shoals the shape
of Lincoln's face, and grave after grave troughed
in the open water. Here is, if life is
a place, just the place to write, and no rage
at the edges, no liaisons where the rocks
and water go at it, wasting time.

                                     Three
thirty. The last mail at five.

                                  "Dear Wilson,
it has come to the attention of the Friends
of Better Books that poetry, mother

of culture, is practiced now (may I be
blunt?) by riffraff elements. The War has
shaken the temple. Ours is to rally
round the bardic mantle where it is worn
with *style*. Would you, to this end, please inquire
what tone Vincent Millay lately takes. Such
an ear! But there are rumors. Use a ruse.
Go disguised as a weekend guest—"

                                        "Listen,
Bunny Wilson, listen good. The maiden
whore is sorry. Edner M'lay is stuck
for an obligatory scene to close
her broken-hearted book, *The Belle on Board:
A Vassar Girl at Sea*. What do you take
for writer's block? Bring me a fifth of it.
(No, wait. A pint is probably enough,
I have it all written in my head.) And ice.
I can't take medicine neat—"

                                "Who is the best?
Me? I am sick to death of burning bright.
Honestly, Bunny, do I have to be
so Godawfully young? The debutante
champagning in a hooped dress, her daybook
tucked in her reticule. I want to write
The Iliad (at least). And you know what's
funny? I'm old. (I know I don't *look* it.)
I need you here, and I will probably
drive you away. Risk it, rabbit.

                                Your bard."

August 5th. Fog.
                6th (7th?). Bright out.
At last. Released from a blank tower, no
nearer the moon. Because a woman's body
is a man's clock (due to the tick of it),
she is the one who takes the time. Bathing
is her reward, a long afternoon's soak.
She is given a tub, a shelf of sponge
and unguents; and when she is not in the bath,

she rubs her wrists and temples with a lily
cologne kept cold in the kitchen by her maid.
She buys it by the case. Also bourbon.

Or so I think (I think too much) today,
swimming alone, afloat, tucked in a wave's
hollow jaw. I wish to be occupied
with just my skin. If anyone calls, I'm
being massaged. Unless it is the boy
Time, threatening a scene. It sets him off
to catch me making up and mirroring.
"Hurry," he says, "our car is here. I *won't*
walk in in the middle, like a tailor
given a pair of tickets by a count
who wants his suits perfect. Your gloves are here.
Your furs. Your fan." Oh, we are off, taking
the corners on two wheels. Nothing is said
about my hair.
                    Tuesday. Bunny accepts.
Jesus.
            The beach. Mumbles and Norma waltz
the slopes, careering down the sand, and lean
shoulder to shoulder to hoot at me. Their hats
are whole umbrellas, and they carry striped
canvas sacks as big as awnings. "Tea time!"
Norma cries. At that, as if hurrahing,
Mumbles' hat takes off to sea, going end
over end, a balloon, a kite. Is it
that I can write it down that I will have
forever mother's face caught in the fast
photograph she makes at the loss of a hat?
Halfway down the dune, her hands on her head,
appalled at the wind's perversity. And glad,
because things have a way of staying on
too long. She huffs over *"Baggage!"* and draws
the line, has always drawn it there.
                                    The tea
is tabled on a beached timber, inches
from the ocean. A tart and biscuits, three
painted cups, and wrinkled, mismatched linen.

Mumbles says that, as we're to have a guest
from The City, we must practice eating
normally, one with another again. We've come
to a pass where a bit of pear and crackers
and a book won't do. "Not for *dinner*. We must
be *rational*," she says, slicing the air
with a spoon. Like old Canute, bellowing "Well?"
over the surf, "What is a little water
to a king?" Our Norma says: "Bunny will think
our meals are like the meals in *Alice*, Ma.
Besides, Bunny is not coming to eat."
We all three titter like spinsters as we pack
our driftwood tea.
               Eleven thirty. Thump.
Someone is bringing a body up the steps
to the porch. The bell. And in comes Bunny, wet
with the night heat: "Christ, it's the lost continent."
He drops his steamer trunk and says, Cockney,
to Mumbles: "Mum, does Edna St. Louis
Missouri live hereabouts?" At midnight
mother produces fish, and now she is
Little Women, radiating gumption
and The Cape Cod Folks. Oh dear.
                  I hound Bunny
with *my* thousand questions about Eng. Lit.
"Like the Eumenides," I tell him.
                     Frown:
"Well, I think you mean the *Sphinx*, don't you?"
                        Hmm.
"Something hungry, then. Fanged. Inquisitive.
And it's got Man's number and eats its young."

One learns to write to write about the years,
one of the Truro sonnets starts. Look at
the second "write." It occupies a place
above the—what?—the fog of sentences
and meaning what is there (when what is there,
if it is true, is far too still to hear).
It doesn't mean, that second "write," *write*. What
am I trying to say? Ah, Bunny knows.

Sunday. Will I marry, he wants to know.
We are throwing shells off Provincetown pier.
I answer lightly, with a line of mine.
No, no, I haven't heard him right. Will I
marry *him?*
          Oh.
               "Oh I can't marry now,
my darling Bunny. Why, I can't thread a
needle, and my mother signed me away
at birth to a mogul. It's out of my hands."
Then, because we are sad, because it is
always better left for another day,
"Give me," I say, "some time. With *two* of us—"
I was going to say the girl's story
stops here, but I don't mean it. It goes on.

Captain Curmudgeon, the man with the cart, halloos,
calling us back, and cuts us short. He's done
the butter-and-egg provisioning for half
Truro, and is the best the village has
in taxicabs. All the way home, Bunny
and I are sailors, keeping the stuff and us
aboard. Some of the time, caught in the ruts
others have wheeled in the way, we click
like a trolley. For the rest, the skipper veers
and blazes a trail, we rattle overland
in fits and starts, and the eggs are on their own.
We disembark at Ryder's field and wait
to watch the captain out of sight, a cloud
of sea birds fanning him off like a sail.

"Would we be the Brownings, Bunny?"
                      Below,
the harbor cups its dream, the going in
and going out only what they are. We
are sea people who do not hold this hill,
this edge, this instant shaped in sand.
                      "You mean,
will I take care of you?"

                    "Oh no. You must
release me from my father's house."
                              "Your father?"
"He is mad. He tells me my paralysis
is fatal. I can do nothing but write."

"Your father's dead. And anyway, you are
a changeling."
                    "Literal Bunny. He's not
really my father. More of a boy, really,
but a tyrant. It's Oedipal as hell."

"Will you marry me?"
                    "Maybe." (*No* is what
I mean, but there you are.) "In the morning
you go back, and I will mull it over."

And that, as they say in the stories, is that.
Or *would* be, but for the moment on this height,
watching the sun go down. We are foolproof
for a little, though the land is running out
like an hour in a glass.
                    Nobody buys
the time in a nice way. It costs the earth.

The Wedding Letter

There's something you don't know about me yet,
and as it separates the charm of lost
innocence from guilt, it is something *you*
ought to know. When we escaped, when we had
witched the witch and come back to the stone town
and learned to wear shoes and tell the hour right
on the tower clock, the burghers' sharp hearts
were in their throats if we were rolling hoops,
you and I, in the cobbled streets. I think
the city fathers dreamed the witch's tricks
had passed to us like a bad cold. The fools.
Practical men, they accounted us some
insurance against the costlier forms
of chaos. The candyhouse in the woods,
they knew, in part is a house in a child's
head. They were beginning to be a race
much kidnapped from, a country for the old
to quarrel for, and so were glad of us,
who rid the world of the magic able
to barter the soul for a ginger snap.
But something else was eating them. We might
get fickle, splash their wives and eldest sons
with warts. To them, a quest was a bargain
that taught you cheaply not to hope next time
that the deep trees beyond the town grow thin
and clear at the gate of a good story.
A moral with no teeth, having been made
to mythologize the bloody fortune
of those few who left us for the wide world
and stayed away and were, notwithstanding
morals, who we wished to be. We didn't
appear *relieved*, you see. It was a blow
to pedagogy and the harder path
of forks and briars. When you come within
an inch of being battered into cakes
and whipped like cream, you should get religion.

The reason I am writing at such length
is to arm you, Gretel. Tonight, as it's
the last before you marry, is the end
of you and me. But go over to them
out of our sleep and slow roses prepared.
They kill their kind, they die like flies, and love
to sing of it, though why they will not say.
They fruit a tart of what they were and throw
a feast to rid them of themselves, then thrill
to the clean, unhungry past they have just
invented, where they will all go soft. Soon
the swords, the swells of pleasure and the gold,
the brave gray stones pelted at the dragon
lie in their custard hearts. Yet to hear them
tell it, they were born realists and not
young and all wrong. Marry. I don't care. But
there is the matter of my gift, which I
am getting to, my yarn, my thread of seeds
to take us back, *my* way out.
                              What a witch
to happen on. Because her secret wish,
to be a girl, was out of her control,
she ate the lost like vitamins, and sinned
as a child sins, with the mouth, the body
not yet real enough to be a weapon.
Why is a witch, if she is open-mouthed,
omnivorous and rich, all skin and bones?
Because what she eats eats her up. Sorrow,
whose stomach is just the size of its eyes,
stands like a broom in her corner. Not to
be lonely, she might have loved us if we
had had a foreign policy and said:

"Our crazy mother threw us in the woods
because of bread. Now we want to settle
in a kingdom made of sugar. You seem
to need an army, with a house this rare.
Compromise. For protection from the poor
and hungry who locust the land, you would

keep us in cookies. We won't want any
mothering, having had our fill of what
the belly does to love."
                              Murder, of course,
is more your sort of sweet. Fast in a cage
and fattened on taffy, I watched you plot
and execute your first crime of passion.
And death, while it is less diplomatic,
has the advantage of pointed fingers.
The nuns never asked which of us jetted
the gas, assuming *I* saved *you*. And then,
coming home is cushioned by a cliché
as well: all is forgiven, have a slice
of bright berry pie, the past doesn't hurt
unless you let it.
                    But you let it. Why?
You shouldered the oven door like an armed
bandit, and the witch drummed her boots on it,
sizzled and wailed, swore to reform, offered
to cook the moon for you. You were as cool
as a firing squad. And when she was done,
the world stirred in its sleep and threw her off.
Her house, it seemed, was a ring of long lost
children, and it fell like a botched soufflé.
The boys and girls were the mortar and bricks,
and they cracked up like a jigsaw puzzle
of gingerbread men, and off they went, whole.
The gumdrops in their faces were their eyes
again. This done, they had no nightmares left.
"Good girl," the forest called, "not guilty. Make
this girl a general."
                      I can see you,
stealing a look at the clockwork cottage
chiming on your mantel. What do you think
being a wife will change? Our first kisses
smacked of ice cream. Maple and vanilla
hung in the air of our sad nursery.
From the first we had a taste for the strange,
biding its time at the edge of the day's
regular appetites. Call it a set

of defenses for murders yet to come
to light. And tonight, more unspeakable
than our secrets is the telling of them.
I went again. (Did you guess what it was,
that it would be *this* that has made of me
a continuous boy, leading a kite
like the town idiot, on a Sunday
flying it by the church while the town prayed,
slow as a planet?) Back to the break in
the spellbound woods, the tulip trees pulling
the bells of their green hours, the chimney crooked
like a finger in the field, and no sign
that a fat house was thought of there in which
the young would hide from time. Only her great
engine of an oven, cool now under
my fingers, had survived the undone trick
of the building. In its belly, on its ashes,
I would take naps while you went off to court
your dancing master. Whatever we were
left alone to practice, I would put down
to get back to my dream, run to the dear
iron room the witch fired her castle in.
And when, one winter day, I brought in hay
to make a bed and saw how I was home,
there came a knocking on the oven door.
It was she.
　　　　　But changed. As young as you
and dressed like a fairy. She had made me
a pastry shaped like a sundial. At each
stroke of an hour, a wave of icing held
a cherry and chopped nuts. A ginger boy
in a chocolate boat was anchored there,
the shadow of his sail telling the time.
The candle in her other hand, she said,
after the pain would leave me free of life
with things to do in a straight town, seeing
they are fatal. *I* would not have to be
a piece of gingerbread. No one would know
from the look of me that I no longer
was involved. And my most secret mission

would be—did you guess?—to follow you.

Poof.

I went up in smoke and woke up a child
forever, far from the rest of you, light
as the paper birds and boxes I hold
high on a string, arrested in the sky.
But I looked like Hansel, and no one knew.

So the past didn't end when you left it,
Gretel, and thus you can't be expected
to be sorry for it. Besides, magic
has other things to be besides a witch.
You weren't that important. That the ice moon
opens again and again is really
no one's fault. It just does. Everyone is
specially scarred by the murder he can't
avoid having on his hands, the killing
by years of one lost child. Go. Go marry
the prince, we want you to. Wear white. The witch,
if anything, is grateful for the push
you gave her into the next mystery.
She speaks of the good luck she plans to rain
on you, who turned her head.

                            All we ask is
that you get us the ground to bless. Banish
the dwarfs appointed to be your royal
furniture. Make the witch your lady's maid,
and she will sit spinning at the window
singing, filtering like the forest shade
the tribes that travel by, the runaways,
the ambiguous garden retreats of
the prince. And I? A jester, a juggler,
whatever the convention is. We three
will play with power safe in the palace.
Servants will come with trays of fresh candy
and stand as still as tables. If they crack
a smile, they forfeit growing old. Or up,
for that matter.

                    Finally, a rumor

of a cure breaks. The line to come inside
snakes with the lame and the colorless out
to the oceans. At our door, where we will love
the best enough to save them, being loved
will stop having its root in what mothers
empty us of because they are starving.

The chance to make us what we were, Gretel.
You can gather the vision you loosed once,
the day you sent the children running home
who had lived in a cake like a coffin
and yet, set free, felt hollow. Like a drug,
sugar scalds if once you take it away.
Every town has one. Out of touch, too
fat, thin in the darks of the eye, shy of
machines.
          Right now, as you read this, the witch
is climbing the tower steps to your room.
Meanwhile, I will guard all the wild candy
stored in the oven. She will lock me in,
she says, to keep me safe. Are you nervous?
You are going to be surprised how much
it is like a mirror, you and she. Yes,
you and she, she says, have always dreamed of
a reunion. Now, as she reaches you,
the wind is filling with flavors, the long
wait ends, and the crumbs gleam in the clearing.
Close as your shadow now. Now she has you
in her charred arms, oh we will be so young.

Musical Comedy

Elyot: That orchestra seems to have a remarkably small repertoire.
Amanda: Strange how potent cheap music is.

—NOEL COWARD, *Private Lives*

TO CÉSAR

May 1935

I

> On the verge of Ohio
> (pray for me)

Cara—
  Well, nothing would have happened if
I hadn't had to pee. But I get bored
sleeping away the night, and getting up
gives me a breath of air. And just lately
I can't get back to sleep. I've always said
there ought to be trains for insomniacs,
special nightlies tooting to Liverpool
and back, with us rocking in little beds
like babies Mum has brandied the gums of.
Trains throw me in comas.
       But not this trip.
I knew it at half-past three. I stood there,
my aim as shaky as a drunk sheriff's,
and thought, What if I have a heart attack,
I bet there's not a drop of digitalis
east of Chicago, once you've left New York.
And then, staring in the itsy mirror
above the sink, I couldn't imagine *what*
went on between Chicago and New York.
A kind of Salisbury Plain perhaps, without
the Druids. I hadn't a clue to the name.
I stood like a misled Genoan, pitched

at earth's edge, wondering where the curve went.
"Good God, man," I said, "see if there's a priest
on board. You want unction." I was rattling
the window down to duck my head out of—
seeking a kind of wind cure—when we stopped.

The night was like a cocktail, mixed and sweet
at the bottom, but there was nothing there
to speak of. Trees and all that, but no *place,*
no station. Goody, I thought, it's bandits.
Or a cow on the tracks. I leaned way out
and could see, because we were on a bend,
the whole of us, end to end, in an arc
like the curl of the new moon above us.
Everything had such—what do I mean?—shape,
I suppose. I'll never sleep again. Naps,
perhaps, but one owes the night an eye
made angry by the day's monotony
and not a lot of idiotic dreams.
Our nannies lied to us about the dark.
Fairies are people-headed after all
and spend a pot of money on their clothes
and wouldn't dance on the head of a pin
unless the press was asked.
                                        What happened was
the thing they tell you not to put in books.
Out of nowhere, a woman in a veil
pearled by the moon appeared, crossing the plain
that seemed a moment since as desolate
as a thin remark of Arnold's. (Matthew
Arnold. Second-rate. A poet trapped in
the body of a boy scout.) I would swear
the moon had thought her up, except for this—
the closer she came to the train, the more
the sky was lit by lost planets so dim
and so far gone that I lost count. The moon
went out, used up in setting the tone. I saw
now, in her coming near, the proper scene
light up. The country depot and the man
who left her, one foot on the runningboard

of his cocoa Packard, his face hidden
in smoke from his cigar. I could have sworn
he was whistling a song I wrote—

A girl who had no elbows stole my heart.
When we danced the tango we were very smart.
But now that I've learned to make love at arm's length,
Everyone's cheek to cheek.

Just then the train
sent up its own soprano, cutting off
the songs the night could carry. She had reached
the tracks, and I had to bend from the waist
into the shivering country air (I don't
wear pajamas, they make me look like George
the Fifth's aunts, all of them), and she got on
and turned in the doorway and parted the veil
(but not so I saw), looking back at him.
They held the moment still between them. This,
I thought, is the way to go—it was clear
they were saying goodbye, that this was it,
and all without a word.
                              Then with a lurch
we went on, and I banged my poor head blue
pulling back in, like a turtle caught out
in a storm. I am a sucker for scenes
in which things done for keeps are given force
by people who have nothing left to lose.
They wear their lizard shoes to the crossroads,
and they get there early so they can pace,
or late and out of breath. Coincidence
is what they're giving up, and thus they plan
the final round down to the fingerbowls.
The things they do with a cigarette
are thicker than the fifth act of *Hamlet*,
and that's before they light it. It may be
love is cheap at making situations,
but what a vehicle for playing dead.

When you come right down to it, what I felt
was, *Christ,* I'm all alone. I didn't say,
but the men on this train—Raskolnikovs,
for the most part, who are beating it home
from college, pistols at their hips—are all,
as *my* aunt said about the *arrivés*
at the edges of her set: "N.O.S.D."
Not our sort, dear.
                If I am to be chaste
coast to coast, I may type my way across.
Americans have never learned to write
anything in twenty minutes, but *I* have.
Backstage, in taxicabs, while cooling soups
in restaurants, I take a phrase to bits
or scribble scenes about mothers-in-law.
Once, standing in line at the bank, I did
a patriotic air. Which reminds me,
I promised you a thing or two to sing
last month. I will be humming it for you,
I promise, when you meet my train. It goes:

> *Where will I be in a year or two*
> *If I get so lost in a day or two*
> *With someone as bloody as you?*

That's as far as I've got. Will write again,
must sleep.
             Oh, in the end I put my head
out the *door* and said to the good captain—
"Where the hell are we?"
                      "Pennsylvania."
Calm as you please. I'm terrified.
                       Love, Noel.

II

Dear Marlene,
             Whoever she is, she's

out of the Packard class. The porter says
the Pullman she's in is *hers*, with its own
liveried staff. It sounds like one of those
gunshy mountainous principalities
teeming with poppies, where the goats are gods.
She stays put. No name. The Madame X bit.
I'll bet my dad's insurance she's a spy,
clicking her infra-red, her ice eyes set,
plotting who knows what scheme for who knows whom.
I'm going in there unarmed. I owe it
to England.
                        Lunch. We will pull in
to Chicago this afternoon. Lilacs
are out in Europe, and they are more real
from where I sit than all this aimless green.
America's too big between the coasts,
so that the trees after a time lose sight
of what they are *vis à vis* the sea. Trees
are all they want to be. Salt is common
only at the table.
                        Which reminds me.
I am supposed to eat a fish that looks
as if a Japanese dried it in sand
to prop it among his pods, sauced with a froth
gone terribly gelatinous. My boiled
potato lies alongside, uninvolved,
like a bar of nice soap. My tablemate,
whom I would as likely have *chosen* as
I would a missionary with a rash
and an eye out for scraps, has told me twice
he is an Indian.
                        "What tribe??" I say.
He looks a bit phlegmy.
                        "Fort Wayne," he says.
Can you picture how bleak *that* place must be,
an old cavalry post, the horses sore
and the souls whored. He certainly seems new
to the real world, or is eating his first
dinner on dishes.
                        3 P.M. What comes

74

of being very bored is never nice,
as the police always say at the scenes
of posh suicides. "Mm," the inspector
remarks, sniffing the tooth glass, "It's like this,
they're sick of being boys, and dying seems
grown-up." It happened between the fish goo
and the heartbroken pudding. My Indian
fulminated. Remarks about his crops,
his tedious roadster, lumps in his lawn,
on his head, in his bed. I clucked and purred
and tried out rhymes in my mind to keep me
busy, when he confessed, "I had it up
before breakfast. I met this crazy girl,
and we did it."
        Did it? When did the tone
alter? I thought we were on to hay ricks
and fields of maize.
        "Don't get me wrong," he said.
"I'm a happily married man."
        "How nice.
Where have you put her? A wife, don't you know,
belongs at a man's side." The squaws, they say,
make blankets all day long and brew green soups
in tents, I've seen it at the pictures. "Ah,
perhaps, the ride on an empty stomach
has lain her low."
        "Eileen? I left her home.
The only thing *she* does in bed is sleep.
I mean a stranger. Nervous. Up all night.
I was having my juice—"
        "Who is she?"
        "Who?
Some whore. She didn't take it off."
        "The veil?"
"They have diseases of the face sometimes.
I don't know. The body was okay. Thin.
She comes in in the middle of my juice,
I was the only one here, and she says—
'Where can I get a whiskey?'
        'I don't know.'

'You want a whiskey?'

                'Now? I want some eggs.'
'*Eggs* aren't going to get you anywhere,'
she says, laughing. Just as if it made sense.
Maybe because she's foreign. All the words
are there, but they don't work. Some women live
in different countries when they speak, with laws
that are only words."

           "Shut up." And I stood,
wild-headed with the countries I had kinged
when she boarded, raving to be her knight,
but certain too that here the enemy
had the advantage of the deep summer
that lies on love's other side. I was here
on the near slope, spring, in the land of good
ideas. "I am a priest. Well may you
snivel and wish now you'd had the omelet,
but that, as the snake said, is applesauce.
People burn for less. Get out."

                "But Father"—
it seems he is an *Irish* Indian—
"I didn't know. You're dressed like—"

                   The red queen's
jack-of-all-whatnot, he might have ventured,
but lacked the accent quite to bring it off.
I can't tell you how indescribable
I looked to him, ascot and suede trousers,
"Celia isn't this party crackerjack"
and all.

          "I'm in disguise," I said,
"doing a hush-hush job. The church today"—
I humphed like Bernard Shaw— "is politicked
and shady as a Baltic state. Anyone
might be—

            but I've talked too much. I must go.
Stay in your room."

              I floated off, seeming
to faint with state secrets. And found her car
next the caboose. The butler at her door
proved firm, but when I said my name, she called

from deep inside to let me pass. I strode
through the beaded curtain into a moor's
pleasure-house, a sort of Persepolis
on wheels. It flashed through me that afterwards
I'd quiz my Indian why he left out
picturing the place. When there she was.
                                        "So you're
Dietrich's writer friend. She never mentioned
you were queer. Are you hungry? You want eggs?"

As easy as that. Festoons, and the floor
all pillows, a big brass table and the cats
on guard from an ivory zoo. And Garbo sat,
a bottle in her hands like Aladdin,
wishing the world away. A face no veil
could put out of focus, whose bones began
in Egypt, then swept west on the spring winds,
and in five thousand years were ready to
resolve themselves as this.
                        "You have whiskey?"

"Sometimes," she said, "before I have breakfast.
Go find a glass."
                So I stood there thinking,
in this W.C. of a kitchen,
"I am getting a glass at Garbo's place,"
larking like an undergraduate. Oh,
the boy's smitten. All for now.
                                Ravished, Noel.

This, P.S., is the doodle that I did
on my napkin. Pardon the fishy bits—

    Oh don't come back, I've had it up to here
    With men whose hearts have vanished in a year.
    I'm all patched up and haven't shed a tear
    In twenty minutes. Oh don't remind me now.

    I'll be all right once you are on a yacht
    Outside the three-mile limit. I have bought

A darling dog who loves me when I'm not
So nice to be with. Oh don't remind me now.

The end is meant to be breathy. La la
love is embers. Down in the throat. No tears.

III

We're just like—
                          sisters, I almost said,
to tease you. Say roommates. In boarding school
over in Provence. Garbo would be the one
who knew, being from New York, how to wear
the hair, whatever the hour, and hitched her skirt
when walking in the hills. The nuns have draped
the mirrors, and the night is corridored
with the whir of bats, and still she pockets
ten quid a week smuggling cigarettes. Help,
sweet Kraut, let me not gush. I can count on
sirens and flags from you, Marlene dear,
who know a fool from a fitful writer
and why he tinkers at people's fences,
because he likes to overlook a field
pocked with hasty choices, wondering what
will grow.
                          We are in Kansas. If you cut
all the grass, you would have the moon. The hills
agree with one another, and they have
no opinion, and no faith in latent
meaning. When we were drunk enough, we found
what was on our minds. I'd sworn off liquor
last month in New York, waking with a nail
driven in my head, having the night before
told my damp producer to mate his dogs
and his daughters. Garbo is something else.
One puts out the lights of resolutions—
nothing tighter than wine, keep pants buttoned,
eschew the parallels to Oscar Wilde—
and lurches round the dark like a lost moth
freed of the dance, mad to let a cottage

in a cardigan. It went like this—
                              "Well,
I hear you write a lot of silly songs.
Do you ever get serious?"
                    "Never.
I do parlor tricks, even in my bath.
I wear a false nose, sometimes pendant from
my right ear. I sleep in the loo, dreaming
of jokes. Who was the man with the Packard?"

"Eric," she said, brushing it off like crumbs.
"You think you're second-rate, don't you? Someone
has to be Shakespeare. Don't you want to be?"

I do not like cushions, sitting as if
I had fallen on ice. I want my tea
at set hours. Dimly, I started to hurt
more than I thought her beautiful (like Keats,
the class item, all his boy's hair sweated
and flat against his head).
                        "Writing is best
kept in its place. It can't be spoken of.
Talk of Shakespeare is an impertinence
to writers. Makes them queasy. One must be
a tonic and potential man, unmarried to
the triple mistress—poems, dreaming, death—
by writing most off the top of one's head.
Eric who?"
                  "You're frightened. They'll laugh at you
if you try a *real* play. Give their tickets
to their servants."
                    "Unfair. It was your move."

This can't be what we said. I remember
we were funny, that we let it be known
we never slept and took to taking turns
at lullabyes.

                  Go to sleep, take a pill,
      We are speeding after the sun, but shh,

We must let him win, the West is his,
And we are only going, going there.

Holding on like orphans of the storm, twined
on a divan in a seraglio, through
the new night, the second night out, Kansas
struggling out of the corners of our eyes
to make it known that sleep lies in the land
and not in our power. After a while,
whiskey washes down like the first hot kiss
of some new pleasure you're not ready for.

What are we going to do? An opera.
We have agreed to write it in one day,
to keep our thoughts in order, for outside
(I tell you this with something like the grief
I had thought was confined to books alone)
the *real* West has begun, prairie (*prairie*,
what a word), and everything seems very
angry and certain.
                              "I hate opera,"
she said, but I said it too. She said: "Why?
Because it takes too long. We'll make something
seriously broken into moments
when you might really sing and say something.
What kind of a name is Noel? English,
ambiguous. The name of a game of cards
or a woollen cape."
                              I must go. I do not,
I should add, say anything but Garbo
and thus haven't said yet what kind *she* is.
Of course I continue to love you.

                                                  Noel.

IV

                              Utah, or perhaps Wyoming. *Somewhere.*

"When you're serious, what do you talk about?"
I asked.
                  "Beauty and time," she said, her arms

behind her head, in men's white pajamas,
the odalisque of the Union Pacific. "Keep love
out of it."
                    "No. You're just being bitchy."
(Eric *appears* to be a no-good boob
whose family's in steel. He dogs her now
and makes her ulcerish. She thought him dear
for about four hours.) "Love is quite profound
in the proper doses."
                    "You do the love songs.
I'll be the naturalist. I want music
an oak tree could whistle to an oak tree.
In fact, I don't want to do people much."

And that is how we began, like the two
Saturday mates, fuzzy in a pub. And one
says to the other, "How do I know I'm
really in love?" And the other one says, "Well,
you put some money down for a wedding ring.
That's real enough."
                    Well, we have just written
two-thirds of something real enough. Garbo,
I don't know why, says not to tell you yet,
but here I go. Keep it under your hat.
Brief synopsis of

            The Boy in the West
        by Noel Coward and Greta Garbo.

Beauty is trapped in the body of a boy
who lives on a leafed and wine-gold coast, muscled
and sunned, watched by his charmed companions three,
a porpoise, a hawk, and a bear, in whom poor Time
is held variously captive, in flux
among all three. The boy sings all day long
about the weather, he sings things *to* it,
boring his even-tempered friends. The hawk,
who tells him what is on the horizon,
sings a song about the cities waiting
to be built beneath them. The bear

keeps the boy in training, is his track coach,
and laments the age of heroes. Last, the gray
whistle-headed porpoise flutes the sun down—
he always has the *soul's* desire at heart.

In Act I, the boy greets the sun at length,
imagining anew the sea-edge seethe
and sea-fall. His design, what he has made
his own, is invisible, as if here
one slept on air, ate air heavy with wet
and honey, no misgivings and no waste.
He touches the place as delicately as
the constant sun in its day-to-day.
                                        And then
the three creatures lecture. Blah-blah, sweetened
(as what isn't) by melody. Today
Time is the hawk, and He is going by.
But suddenly (finally) some sails are sighted.
(Every comedy is so like *The Tempest*,
it has to have a Miranda living a life
there, as well as an Ariel, who's queer.)
And they let off little boats that dimple
to the land of The Boy in the West, who sings,
"Come, there is so much room for us here."
                                        Horns.
Twenty or so Dickensian folk appear,
all criminals, a whole court plot against
a king, brought to exile. Flowers alone
they exempt from their hatred of outdoors.
They *loathe* country life. Bringing up the rear,
their warden, a pretty girl (unarmed), who sings,
"Notice the light. It is so *light* here, like
a dream."
                        They catch sight of one another.

Act II.

The Bleakhouse Gang, onstage,
do a rousing number while they cut trees
and start their suburban villas. The boy,

having for love of her lost track of Time,
brings the girl back here to his harbor reach—
she has made him put on a woven cloth
over his privates (most fetching)—and sees
the hack work happening and moans.

                                 "Stop them!"
he sings. "They will trust you."

                                 "What's wrong?"
she wonders. "We are building a new world."
(In a comedy you write about being
happy, for which there are no images,
and the people in it disagree a lot.)
"Wrong!" rings out of the sky and up the beach
and then booms in the hills. Three lost voices
chorusing what's gone wrong. The hawk rides in
on the bear's brown shoulder, shrieking. Time itself,
he says, has brought this on, to ruin those
who hold Him to a form. No, says the bear,
for Time is over. They none of them hear
the clear kazoo of the porpoise, swimming off,
Time locked in his heart like a man in a boy,
trying to say that Beauty and Time will cease
to coexist. "Otherwise," he murmurs,
"nothing will change."

                       What can the poor girl do?
She's bound by law to civilize the place,
to make it St. Tropez. "We can't stop it,"
she sings, "but we will make it beautiful."
The Boy in the West, for love of her, agrees,
though Beauty, reading Proust in Her apartment
in his heart, can't abide the adjective
traded under Her name, and shuts Her book.

Once the boy yields, the wilderness latent
in everything comes true. The bear rumbles
and practices mauling. The hawk's good eye
turns to the dumb nut-gatherers who lunch
in the open. This is all done in a trio
in which the wordless fury that man can't
talk his way into is called back in—hawk

and bear and, faintly, the beep and toot from the sea
where the porpoise has tried to flee with Time.
"Growl" goes the world. Time is no longer held,
not one thing and not another. The boy,
for love of her, is deaf. The curtain falls.
When I am with her, Marlene, I feel
like Nora running away with Hedda.
I feel like I am coming to summer.
Of all the passages that I have made,
I have not won this one. Ironic, that.
I am the great writer of shipboard romance.
I will be in L.A. at nine thirty
tomorrow, in the A.M.

                    Ta ta, Noel.

V

Lili M.—
          I am writing a fifth time
to separate what's gone from what's gone on.
No time to post it. There isn't a place
between here and there. I'll hand it to you,
you can read it later. You won't like it.

It started with (everything does, in a way),
"Let's go to bed."
                    "But we won't sleep," I said,
dead at the piano. We had written
two acts in fourteen hours, right on schedule,
and said let's break to catch our breath. Outside,
a desert warred with a stack of mountains.
                                        "No,
I mean let's fuck."
                    "Don't be perverse. I don't
go with ladies."
                    "So what? Sometimes I drop
an egg in a whiskey, raw. It doesn't mean
I've given up ice. Is it very small?"

*

"What? My thing? It depends. Don't be lurid.
Or intimate. You won't budge a button."

"I thought we were getting serious."
                                        "Did you?
It is a word you use far too often,
the way an Eskimo might say 'fish.' We are
getting our sea legs. Getting West. *I* thought
we were after loftier things than us."

The line of that mouth. Like a line on a map
drawn from Caesar's to Cleopatra's city,
the distance between two points, just as Shaw saw,
but with the added weight of the going there.
One knows what Garbo means before she speaks.

"I want to be alone for a while. You're right
about one thing. I know my way around
a ship. I'm built like Popeye. Do you mind?"

"No no," I said. "I'll get my things together."
(I'd not been in my room since Illinois.)
"There ought to be a proper interval
before Act III, so we can pee and fix
our faces. Ta."
                        Speedy exit. Foxtrot
from car to car, the homeless boy, coursing
the badlands under someone else's steam,
no stops. What is it the knight feels, riding,
when he can no longer make out the scarves
billowing from her tower? That he must
keep the tower now for his destiny,
his life a circle meant to bring him back.
The queen can be The Beginning till he moves.
The least movement changes her into The End.
That is how quests are undergone.
                                        In my room,

85

of all people, the Indian lay fast
asleep. Well well. His sheep eyes popped open,
and he went into the Emily Post routine
Americans are dreariest at. "Gee whiz,
Father, I must have fallen off." Brilliant.
"I feel so bad, I've mussed your bed."

                             "Tell me,
what are you here for?"

                             "I want to confess."
The ensuing scene, the deleted scene, is pure
pornography. Cut. Not because you can't
take the facts. More because we must be free,
as I pull in, of the diversions of
the *entr'acte*. Likewise, facts are not comic
or musical, and one bit of singing
remains to sound, thin as the porpoise's kiss.
I mention the Indian at all to prove
everyone sleeps in the end with everyone else,
though not onstage. He proves our pain is not
carnal. Garbo and I were both *satisfied*,
as far as that goes.

                      How long does it take
to bring these things to a head? Perhaps an hour.
Two at most. It's true, we dozed off. I woke.
It was dark. I left him and all my things
and sprinted east. Oh wait.

                           She was waiting,
veiled, outside our Aladdin's car. She seemed,
in the no-man's-land between two coaches, lost
to us and our faith in places. She'd flung wide
the door, and the night rushed us, longing to fan
her face.

               "Good. I wasn't going to wait,"
she said, "but now you'll know. I finished it.
The bear kills the girl. The boy kills the bear.
The hawk plummets, aiming right for his eyes.
The boy as he's blinded cracks the hawk's wings.
All of their ghosts sing at the end."

                             "I see.
and the porpoise?"

"Drowns. He doesn't sing a note
in Act III. Too upset. Excuse me."
                              Then
she reached behind my head and yanked a cord,
and bells rang and lights flashed. We slowed and slowed.

"What did you do that for?"
                              "I have to go."

And so we stopped. I don't know where we were.
We were in clouds, no a fog but wet, drenched
with the air that clings around mountains.
                                        "Really,
don't leave, I mean I don't care what we are,
but dammit—"
                    "This has nothing to do with *you*.
It's that Eric expects me in L.A.
done up like a slave girl. This is his train,
you know. It's his whole damn *railroad* we're on.
He buys silly people by the carload. You see,
you have to be serious just to breathe.
Goodbye. We'll meet again. The same people
are after us both."
                        Ah but don't you see,
what if they get me first? I'm going west,
and I can't keep it straight which way is up.
I'll be awake, the stars will be about,
and the strange, traveling lover that rides in me
will never come back. Forgive me. I've come
to think some places are the songs we sing.

"Where is *The Boy in the West*?"
                                    "I threw it out."
"It's half mine. I want it."
                                "I threw it out
the *window*. The wind took it. You don't need it."
The train jerked and began, and she leapt down.
Oh I am an oak whistling after an oak.
I leaned out, and the train blew the veil up
just enough for the full moon in her eyes

to pass from cloud to cloud. And we held still,
though The Wild West Show rolled on, this way and that.

John Donne, our great comic actor, has a prayer
written on a horse—I mean, while he was
riding. And he's traveling west because
he can't bear his muse (in his case it's God),
because it makes him laugh when he would cry
about Beauty, and how It just goes out.
I have been alone about two hours now,
so I will be all right if there's the press
wanting to know who my characters are
in *real* life, as if there could *be* real life
as time-bound as a play. In just two hours,
you can watch Prospero go back to town.

At least I have got the right thing for you.
Here is a serious song I wrote today,
the love left out of it. I'm not afraid
of L.A. the way I am of New York.
Here, I know, a spade is a spade and not
a heart. Sing this for what in us is still
lost in transit.

Home on the Southport Car.

My father came home on the Southport car,
A kind of club for commuting men.
It took them home to Connecticut
And back each day to New York again.

He wasn't much more than a banker then,
Not as rich as a man in stocks,
But he showed a great flair for backgammon
On the Southport car, where there are no clocks.

A lovely man. And I had a horse,
And my mother a mink that was a miracle.
On Friday nights they went out to dine.
And he did get a raise. That's empirical.

So why fall in love on the Southport car,
When you can do it at the Plaza?
Once you have read your Henry James,
You want to know first where the bars are.

But he fell in love with a journalist
Whose pieces appear in the New York World,
A man of alarming ancestry,
An Irishman, his hair all curled.

Now they are both intellectuals,
And they have a place on the coast near Rome,
And the Southport car goes back and forth,
But it does not bring my father home.

The Carpenter at the Asylum

(1975)

To MVM and Ridgely

Things floating like the first hundred flakes of snow
Out of a storm we must endure all night,
Out of a storm of secondary things . . .

—WALLACE STEVENS

October in Massachusetts

TO EM PRESTON

No good at knowing what tree it is, I see
one keeping green this long, notice such
deliberate inconsistencies only because

I'm writing to you. The apple and pumpkin man
makes daily trips in his pickup down our street.
Neighbors are covering mums against frost. I

enter fall without jobs and devices, carry out
September like a dog stoned by rough boys, now
homing, clotting up, called to, waiting out

a healing in someone's hands: I plan winter
trips instead. I would rather, gathering chestnuts
and bittersweet, know a greed for autumn daylight.

The sea breezes across Amalfi over the tombs
are not such special cures. Even the rainforest
in Puerto Rico is small as a state park.

Anyway, Em, it's a poem I've meant to write
all year. We get too busy, it seems, to make
a common reason for the truth. But the version

of me that you are, rushed, kept close like
spare plans, is the one I'd stay for, that no
weather measures, that I can't travel out on,

and writes no excuse for an autumn month:
October's just October, its twilight feel,
its way of dying out something to invent.

When I am with my friends, I can describe
leaves piling like anybody: I've hid my losses
in those brief lies. So the warm air seeps

*

from the city, another kind of version for
another kind of season. We weather winter well
seven weeks before Christmas. In January we

remember a sugar maple's fire with the same
inadequate names I miss you with. Only because
I love you, Em, I travel on winter names.

Paris Days

It doesn't mean a thing, in a way, to be here.
My poor-luck uncle lived eight years on this
street and can't recall just why, he badmouths

Paris now and reads Tacitus if he's drinking.
He weeps his dull, later tears. Tatterdemalion
all this week, I stir like late-flown banners

and undo all my meanings, fooled by another
longing as a zoo of soft-footed animals. I read
nothing of the sort myself. Near me at breakfast

a Pennsylvania mother mulcts her irregular verbs.
My tour is much the same device, I stroll my
way. The grubby, distended city I inhabit not

fully left behind, I shy like a chatty teacher
puzzled in his room. I've said all this before,
he thinks, and no one in his class expects it

otherwise, all the same it's sad. I marvel that
the predators are coquettish in my dreams, eat
legumes and ripe greens, paw and lope the swamp

acres of their home ground, the havoc out of it,
the trees green. The restless, big-shouldered cats
cast their feathers and old fur deep in the ruts

of a dying time. I gawk at Paris like a king's
explorer out to get monkeys and blue parrots,
wigged and rather balmy on a Congolese plateau.

II

Art is not a substitute. Still, street dancers
flip their foul caps in cocksure animation, do
what they do to track and shuttle money, crafted

as an absolute occasion. Its imminent repose
holds the city guardedly this evening. I'm off
at a wander pace to flee the heat in the Roman

museum, skirting pale relic laces and stuccos
for the unicorn panels. I make up their laconic
history: a woman sells her twin children, boy

and girl, to a Norman guild. She breaks their slim
knees with her fish rake, binding them over young
to a Flemish carpetman. They only cry at first.

They weave in a cell for years their spinners'
rhythms, and when they fall in love, they ache
and jubilee their lucent skin. At rest their mad

arms cover each other like beaten garments. Months
they work on the otter and frail lion attending
her spinnet, her sensuous tent and standard. Every

fiber of her mild look is sewn in repose. Rising
herons and cheetahs lift like a trellis behind
her. The tetanus rim on the garden wall threatens

the world without. This world. Working forty
years they only reach the pearling muscles under
the beast's immaculate neck. In the nineteenth

century, ruthless nuns stitched over the tray
of glazed persimmons from the south. I expect
another day for my corrosion, cooling off after

a run, and on the forest floor I see the swift
shine of his mane. I flounder or seize the air,
but as I stand he leaves his whiskey sting in me.

The hothouse aroma of grapes and sultanas fills
the drear wood. The unicorn gathers his wand like
a quiver of Arab thread. The air is incredible.

III

My letters are rife with small excursions
taken savagely. Busy still with details, I
would sit down now and let the clouded dark

sail in. Forfeiting even this—they will not
shrug their crutches—the gaudy beggars reel
off their random dangers for a penny, empty

of intent, and thank no one. In the king's
ballroom, his women carry cricket cages at
the waist, dazzled by them mourning near.

Stayed in an upper gallery, the attenuated
men of Crete on the salon walls give up their
bent weapons to other men, all of them slick

and mythic as the satin spaces of their skin.
Surrendered, piping still, fires out under
the lambs, some are in tombs, some attended

at night by nurses in masks. The frequent
instrument of time arrests us in its gleam
and strange measure. Packing up, I sort what

goods I've purchased and will store away. I
jot down in the taxi how long the flowers
linger. Hold back this loss too. I feel in

this day's stupid chill the dream that I ring
down, image within image. In Rembrandt's late
self-portrait, head bound in a rag, he says:

if I have fabricated this, then tell me why
I feel like I'm diving fearfully among these
ravening stars that skate here in my eyes.

Janis Joplin's Death

SAN JUAN, JANUARY

At a hundred two the cook's mother is oldest,
daughter of a midisland caneworker and her dwarf
brother. This is a matter of fact. She eats fried

sweet dough and feels good this Three Kings' Day.
The Las Cabézas beach is weed-sifted, damp
for this day's party. We dig roast pits early

and wait out dusk, the children claim the water.
I am too tired out to be here, where I would rather
be: word comes here daily how they are dying.

At eighty-five degrees the sun is used to me:
how I plan to last, I think. Now, hearing them
die off, I look for any clue, here where the

Andalusian captains chalked their bad maps,
forty miles east of the forts. Late troop boats
seek anchor in this blue bay. Palm-shadowed,

the conquerors, come around the jetty end, clamor
for this water. They home in, strip their gilt
and complicated suits and brass-mail skirts. Oh,

they swim like something done with living. Unhoisting
their amazing sails, the last sailor rides with them.
They roll slow, floating, calming down in this

trip's finish. I hear they are dying back home.
In the coastal towns, the priests bale old toys
for the city poor, they bring in the Host to ones

too sick for Three Kings' mass. The governor's
flown home for the weekend. Who first told me,
I wonder, how we sketch a marvelous projection

*

in our time? Loosening ourselves this way, we own no holiday. The harbors aren't gained. Tomorrow morning we sail out early. We get lost fast.

Contexts

For David Schorr

You probably won't be needing whatever
it is you thought to bring, and besides
you won't be judged by the baggage you

carry. You have to get out of here fast.
Becoming a poet, and poets will often
deceive you about it, hasn't to do with

grandiloquent symbols. Some strut about
the decks obscurely, awaiting the call
like halfwit neurasthenics on vacation.

Every time they talk, the word outlives
the idea, its tentative size diminished
and taken apart like shipwreck, waste

and runic. You sit alone and worry your
oar, in tense accommodation, an alien
mystic fallen among chance captains.

Wayward tribes have settled these rural
borders badly, fastening trivial tents
in regular rows. We will not have it,

we are a runaway crowd, I assure you,
ranging in barbarous places. Vanish,
then, to begin with. The quest, if that

is what it is, is differently laid out
than balladeers have mentioned. You are
walking outdoors with a friend, avoiding

your letters. It could happen to anyone:
something—a beetle, a snake sliding out
of the shrubbery—bites him. Maybe you

call for help, but the bridges are out
or the road's dismantled, and nobody's
coming for hours. You prop him up, talk

about meaningless things, thus conspire
against the dazes and wildering spell
of dying. Ply him with insular legends

and omens and obsolete miracles. You'll
not outwit its imminent looming, yet
play for an hour a secluded music done

with time. There is where you are going.
All men are finally stricken, the poison
takes, their agreeable faces shrivel. In

the best of their snakebite songs we've
delivered the vision intact. Keep watch
for the singular passage. Be casual. Out

of sight of land and about to surrender,
you arrive without warning at a languid
shoreline and smile as if nothing at all

had ended. Olives crown the headlands,
and a raging orchid carpet rings these
slopes like arrogant starfire. Ambiguous

phrases that blur in the tropical air
like spice and pollen order themselves
superbly. Your most precipitous guesses

are pooled and cycled in seconds as epic
and rhyme besides. You can do anything.
The surf will as usual prosper, its lift

and leisurely slap continue: that is all
anyone knows of the rhythm of things. Go
scout a more subtle system than the sea,

ignore for once its predictable singing.
Myself, I hollowed beachfruit for hours
the first morning, watching its colorless

meat disperse like failing daylight. Or
lower your barrels and mine the shallows
for ancient loot, or relish the marvelous

shapes of the floor. The words will come
later. The pipestem fish come hauling
for you now, the direst insects zing on

the green ridges. Getting it on the page
is automatic, and you risk a small sorrow:
if no one will believe you, you may be

stranded by fevers and foolish jewels in
that still harbor. But never mind. Go
anyway, just for the castaway harmonies.

Listen, I would be lying if I pretended
that critics will not matter, but if you'd
travel faster, believe it. And take care:

one does not ask why we do it. The words
our lips could master would make us all
human if we knew them. That, and the pain.